"What comes to replace and improve upon the idea of identity for a world of emergence, flux and multiplicity? What is the reference point for self-regulating processes in our complex systems? The answer is eigenvalues. In this exemplary work of study between disciplines, where science and art meet and cross-pollinate, Hanjo Berressem has given us the most thorough and inspirational explanation of one of the hidden keys to modern life."

James Williams, Honorary Professor of Philosophy, Deakin University, Australia

"Hanjo Berressem's *Eigenvalue* is a bold new approach to the theory of the technological and the political unconscious, one that is not centered on the individual. *Eigenvalue* is structured as two explorations in book form—one on science, and one on the arts. Ranging across quantum physics, cybernetics, and chaos theory in the first book, to Alvin Lucier on the acoustic unconscious, Bill Morrison on the visual unconscious, and Thomas Pynchon on narrative literature in the second, Professor Berressem both illustrates the resonance across science and poetics and develops extremely important new theoretical contributions to studies of the unconscious."

David Holdsworth, Associate Professor, Trent School for the Environment, Canada

Eigenvalue provides the first history of the term "eigenvalue" by building an important bridge between the hard and the soft sciences. Originally a mathematical term, Hanjo Berressem applies eigenvalue, which roughly translates to "proper value," to the media studies discipline for the first time, providing a philological history and line of development across the sciences through to contemporary cultural studies. Berressem's groundbreaking work is organized into two books, with the first book broken down into six topical areas—mathematics, physics, cybernetics, biology, literary studies, and cultural studies. The second book discusses the place of eigenvalues in music, film, and literature; specifically, Alvin Lucier's experimental composition "I am Sitting in a Room," Bill Morrison's eight-minute experimental film *Light is Calling*, and the literary works of Thomas Pynchon. Berressem's thought-provoking philology is an important reference point for readers seeking an authoritative introduction to a term that connects other key ideas in contemporary debate.

Hanjo Berressem is Professor of American Literature at the University of Cologne, Germany. His publications include *Pynchon's Poetics: Interfacing Theory and Text* (1993) and *Lines of Desire: Reading Gombrowicz's Fiction with Lacan* (1998).

thinking|media

Series Editors:
Bernd Herzogenrath
Patricia Pisters

EIGENVALUE

On the Gradual Contraction of Media in Movement

Hanjo Berressem

BLOOMSBURY ACADEMIC

NEW YORK • LONDON • OXFORD • NEW DELHI • SYDNEY

BLOOMSBURY ACADEMIC
Bloomsbury Publishing Inc
1385 Broadway, New York, NY 10018, USA
50 Bedford Square, London, WC1B 3DP, UK

BLOOMSBURY, BLOOMSBURY ACADEMIC and the Diana logo are
trademarks of Bloomsbury Publishing Plc

First published in the United States of America 2018

For legal purposes the Acknowledgments on p. vii constitute an extension
of this copyright page.

Cover design: Daniel Benneworth-Gray
Cover Image © Paolo Sanfilippo

A catalog record for this book is available from the Library of Congress.

ISBN: HB: 978-1-5013-3518-1
ePDF: 978-1-5013-3520-4
eBook: 978-1-5013-3519-8

Series: thinking|media

Typeset by RefineCatch Limited, Bungay, Suffolk
Printed and bound in the United States of America

To find out more about our authors and books visit www.bloomsbury.com
and sign up for our newsletters.

CONTENTS

READER'S MANUAL

The form of this book, with its two "back-to-back" sides, owes something to a publishing practice that was especially popular in America during the 1950s and 1960s. Two novels, mostly science-fiction or crime novels, were published back-to-back, the idea being to give the reader "two novels for the price of one." When books were published in that way, they had banners on their respective covers that advertised the extra novel, such as "turn over for second book," which, in my case, would have to read "turn over for second study." A difference between such books and this book, which uses that back-to-back form to express the complementarity of and the resonances between the scientific and the artistic aspects of the originally mathematical term "eigenvalue," is that although the two sides can be read "on their own," the reader is also free to move, at any given point, from one side to the other.

Eigenvalue: On the Gradual Contraction of Media in Movement provides a philological and conceptual history of the term "eigenvalue." In 20th century science, from mathematics, physics and cybernetics to literary and media studies, the term is used to conceptualize "processes of formation" within media multiplicities. The history of the term provides a framework for the analyses of the three case studies on the other side of the text. – Turn over for second study.

ACKNOWLEDGMENTS

Work on "this side" started, not that I knew it at that moment, with a question I had in the spring of 2011, shortly before teaching a seminar on American autobiographies. In a text on the "selfbiography", Wilhelm Dilthey had used the term "eigenvalue," which I didn't know, and I wanted to have an answer ready in case students asked me about the term's meaning. Although I did some "last minute research," I felt lucky that none of the students wondered about the term. During the following years, the text accrued, slowly but persistently, around this "primal scene."

The writing took me, often quite unexpectedly, into conceptual fields that I was not familiar with at the time, and many of which I still find extremely daunting, such as linear algebra, quantum physics or cybernetics. I have tried to work myself into these fields as best I could, and I have talked to a number of people who know more about them than I ever will, such as Moritz Ingwersen or Burak Sezer. If there are, despite their good advice, mistakes in this text the fault is all mine, and I apologize. Those are the challenges, I guess, but also the fascination of interdisciplinary research.

There are a number of people without whom the text would never have been finished. Nadine Boljkovac-Berressem, Jasmin Dücker, Julius Greve, Björn Sonnenberg-Schrank, Eleana Vaja, Verena Wurth and my brother Jürgen Berressem read the text at various stages, providing invaluable feedback, criticism and encouragement, as well as working tirelessly against my deplorable inability to provide exact references and complete bibliographical data.

I also want to say "thank you" to Bloomsbury's readers, David Holdsworth, Sascha Pöhlmann and James Williams. Not only because of their admirable expertise in both the hard and the human sciences, one could not have found better minds to trust with the text. They looked the text over with in many ways undeservedly favorable eyes. If they were kind enough to see merit in a project that might be considered to be somewhat arcane, so were Bernd Herzogenrath and Patricia Pisters, in whose series this text has found a wonderful home.

The same goes for Bloomsbury, who published the text in the way I envisioned it from the moment of its conception. Special thanks go to Katie Gallof and Erin Duffy who, despite many obstacles, made the design of this book possible.

A different kind of thanks is due to the people who suffered through the writing of the book in all kinds of scholarly weather: exasperated, unusually talkative, eerily absent, not-to-be-disturbed, moody, or "on some other planet entirely." These thanks go out to my kids, Keyla and Dahlia, who got used to Dad "working away" or being "lost in thought." Finally, my love and gratitude go out to Nadine "mydinny" Boljkovac-Berressem, who makes life good in all kinds of weather, scholarly and otherwise.

INTRODUCTION

Let me begin with a number of *caveats* about this book. I am neither a scientist nor a historian of science. Having come to the hard sciences through literary studies, I cannot fully judge the truth-value of the scientific theories I deal with. On this level, therefore, my text cannot be "critical." Also, all of what I am going to say about the single sciences' use of the term "eigenvalue" [*Eigenwert*] has been said in these sciences in much more depth and detail. Finally, I do not claim that the theory of eigenvalues can explain the world and the way it functions. In this respect, this book is quite useless. Compared with the many books that claim, with admirable conviction, that they do know how the world functions, my aim is much more humble. All I want to do is trace the incarnations of the term eigenvalue in various fields of knowledge, from mathematics to cultural studies, and to show its presence in and implications for the field of media studies. If this tracing sometimes leads me to describe in detail moments that seem at first sight to be quite out of the way and far from each other, I hope the reader will bear with me.

Generally, I see my task as philological rather than as scientific. In fact, I know of the term eigenvalue only because it has migrated from the hard sciences into literary studies, which is where I first picked it up. As a German, I of course knew the word "eigen," translated, amongst others, as "proper," "singular," "distinct," or "unique," which is a very common component of compounds such as "*eigenartig*," which means "peculiar," "*eigenbrötlerisch*," which denotes a psychic state somewhere between "weird" and "asocial," "*eigensinnig*" or "*eigenwillig*," which designate slightly different versions of being "stubborn," "*eigenverantwortlich*," which means to be "responsible for oneself," and "*eigentlich*," as "in actual fact." "Eigen" is also used in compound nouns such as "*Eigentum*," which means property, as in "*Eigenheim*," which denotes one's own small house. Ulrich, the protagonist of Robert Musil's novel *The Man without Qualities* [*Der Mann ohne Eigenschaften*], is in a constant state of potentiality, but also without anything that marks him as in any way "specific." He has no characteristics [*Eigenschaften*].

Even before the terms "eigenvalue" and "eigenfunction" were invented by the German mathematician David Hilbert, the German language and the human sciences were permeated by reference to "eigenhood" and to "the eigen." The first section of the second part of Max Stirner's 1845 book *The Ego and His Own* [*Der Einzige und sein Eigentum*] "Ich," for instance, is called "the eigenhood" [*die Eigenheit*]. In the context of the description of his anarcho-individualistic philosophy, Stirner uses, with almost excessive exuberance, a large number of eigencompounds, in particular *Eigentum* [property] and *Eigenheit* [individual characteristic: ownness]. Most importantly, he defines the individual as *der Eigene.* The semantic ambiguity of "*eigen*" denoting that somebody or something is singular and unique but also peculiar or "queer" also reverberates through the name of the world's first gay journal, which was published by Adolf Brand in Berlin between 1896 and 1932. In direct reference to Stirner's anarcho-individualism, it was called *Der Eigene.*

Because the word "eigen" is so common in German compounds, its own eigenvalue is often overlooked, except when it occurs in new compounds such as eigenvalue, which I first noted while teaching a course on life writing. Part of the course's theoretical apparatus was Wilhelm Dilthey's essay "Experience and the Selfbiography" ["*Das Erleben und die Selbstbiographie*"], which was written between 1907 and 1910 and published in 1927 (*Schriften, VII*, 191–204).

In that essay, Dilthey, who coined the term "human sciences" [*Geisteswissenschaften*] that set the category of understanding or sense and thus the peculiarity [*Eigengesetzlichkeit*] of the human sciences, against the category of knowledge defining the hard sciences, uses the term to differentiate between unconsciously *lived*, consciously *experienced*, and artistically *recorded* life.

Dilthey's essay is the primal scene of this book. It was in trying to make sense of Dilthey that I became aware of the presence of the term "eigenvalue" in mathematics, literary studies, physics, cybernetics, systems theory, biology, and cultural studies. Reading up on the term's complex history, I was surprised how seamlessly Dilthey's philosophy of life [*Lebensphilosophie*] could be aligned with the logic of eigenvalues as it was developed and used in the hard sciences. I hope that chapter 5, which will return me to Dilthey on the background of the history of the term that I will have assembled by that point, evokes some of my initial wonder, the primary affect that marks the beginning of interest and thus of any form of science, philosophy, and art.

Along its historical vector, the term accumulates its own logic and an adherent argument. It is charged with more and more meanings and connotations and it develops a cloud of derivatives, such as "eigenfunction," "eigenfrequency," "eigenoperation," "eigenspace," "eigentime," "eigenrhythm," "eigenbehavior," "eigenorganization," and "eigenworld;" a term proposed by Ludwig Binswanger in his 1946 essay "The Existential Analysis School of Thought" to denote one part of the triad of *Umwelt* (the environment), *Mitwelt* (the communal world), and *Eigenwelt* (the personal, or "proper world"). Binswanger took these three modes of existence from Martin Heidegger, who had talked, in his lectures of the 1919–20 winter semester, of *Umwelt*—a term originally coined, together with those of *Merkwelt* and *Wirkwelt*, by Jakob Johann von Uexküll—*Mitwelt*, and *Selbstwelt* (self-world) (*GA*, 58, 33, ff), and who had defined the *Lebenswelt* (life-world) as the superposition of these three domains (34, ff). In the 1980s, Cornelius Castoriadis takes up the notion of "eigenworld" in relation to the logic of "autonomy" (9) as understood by "my friend Francisco Varela" (337). While the English translator David Ames Curtis uses "proper world," he also notes that "[t]he term 'proper world' may easily be understood in English on analogy with 'proper name.' Thus, also, 'proper organization,' 'proper time,' and so on" (xxxv). In fact, later in *World in Fragments* "proper time" is given as "(*Eigenzeit*)" (385). Already here: a vector from eigenvalue to eigenworld.

What, very roughly, is an eigenvalue? Today, the term is commonly used to designate "intrinsic value" or "value in itself" [*Eigenwert*] as opposed to what Karl Marx called "use value" [*Gebrauchswert*]. As Immanuel Kant noted in the second principle of his categorical imperative, "[a]ct in such a way that you treat humanity, whether in your own person or in the person of any other, never merely as a means to an end, but always at the same time as an end" (*Grounding*, 36).

If one extends Kant's imperative to the realm of the non-human, a natural object such as a plant, an animal, or nature in general have an eigenvalue, as opposed to the particular use value they might have for a specific owner, industry or culture, what in German is called *Fremdwert* ["value for others"]. As such, the term sets the value of an object in and of itself against its functional value for somebody else. It stakes its "givenness" against its "givenness as given" to and for somebody. Ecology, for instance, stakes the eigenvalue of natural objects and animals against their industrial exploitation, arguing that no living or even non-living being, such as a rock formation, should ever be reduced to the value it has for others. As Arne Naess notes in "The Deep Ecological Movement: Some Philosophical Aspects," "[t]he well-being and flourishing of human and non-human life on Earth have value in themselves (synonyms: intrinsic value, inherent value). These values are independent of the usefulness of the non-human world for human purposes" (68; see also "Deep Ecology," 130).

Although I will also touch upon the ecological, my review of the historical unfolding of the term will in the first instance develop what might be called an "eigenargument" about the term as an important reference *for* and *in* media studies, where it has led a mostly unnoticed existence in the context of the fundamental distinction between medium and form. While the former is assumed to have no eigenvalue, the latter is assumed to have one. What the term's history will show, however, is that this distinction is more complicated than it is generally considered to be. My argument, which "assumes" this complication, takes up, from within the logic of eigenvalues, Gilles Deleuze's notion of contemplation and contraction. "What organism is not made of elements and cases of repetition, of *contemplated and contracted water*, nitrogen, carbon, chlorides and sulphates, thereby intertwining all the habits of which it is composed?" (*Difference and Repetition*, 75, emphasis added). In analogy, I will argue that forms are contracted and contemplated media, while media are dissolved and dispersed forms. There is a complementarity between media and forms, that is, not a distinction. Perhaps the term "eigenmedium," which is a contradiction in terms, might express some of that paradoxical complementarity.

The form of the book takes up this complementarity. It is meant to align two projects that are written from within a media studies perspective, and to underline the deep affinity and resonance between them. One project is to write a history of the term "eigenvalue," the other is to show the presence of the term in the arts.

The titles of the book's "two sides" take up Deleuze's terms. Although they are complementary and thus cannot be separated except in a formal sense, this side stresses the contraction of media. It is the more scientific and theoretical one. The other side, which is the more artistic and practical, stresses their contemplation. My hope is that the "two sides" will illuminate each other and form, together, a topology of thought that is adequate to the book's topic. At the same time, each side can be read on its own.

Parts of the text have been published previously, in different form or language, as "'The Habit of Saying I': Eigenvalues and Resonances" and as "'Der *Eigen*name': Eigenwert und Eigenbiographie." All translations from German titles are mine.

Chapter 1

MATHEMATICS: 1904

In his book *Wissen und Gewissen*, Heinz von Foerster notes that the German mathematician David Hilbert introduced the neologism "eigenvalue" into the field of linear algebra "around the turn of the century" (241, see also Segal, 146). More precisely, Hilbert first introduced the term—together with the term "eigenfunction" [*Eigenfunktion*]—in his 1904 essay "Grundzüge einer allgemeinen Theorie der linearen Integralgleichungen (Erste Mitteilung)," in which he states that "[p]articularly in this first note [*Mitteilung*] I reach formulas that provide the development of an arbitrary function according to specific distinguished functions that I call Eigenfunctions" (51). Hilbert adds that "[w]e introduce here the following designation: the roots of δ (λ) shall be called the eigenvalues that belong to the kernel (s,t)" (64).

In linear algebra, eigenvalues are used to describe transformations— defined as processes in which "operators" H(x) describe specific programs or routines, such as "the action of H on x"—that concern the shape and the orientation of vectors within a vector space. For instance, if one plots a turbulent movement within a vector space, it will show a multiplicity of random, inherently unsystemic and unperiodic vectors, or perhaps more precisely, points, that emerge and vanish "almost instantly," as in the image of white noise on "a television tuned to a dead channel." If one plots a vortical movement, in which minimally formed vectorial systems have emerged from a state of pure turbulence, it will show a minimum of order and stability, and thus systematicity. At the moment when the dynamics shift from turbulence to vortex, the points begin to show a first, "infinitely faint" communal orientation. In other words, as Michel Serres notes in *The Birth of Physics*, while turbulent space is "simply disorder" (28) and thus movement without form, vortical space contains "a particular form in movement" (28). Lucretius' notion of the *clinamen* in *De Rerum Natura*, to which Serres refers, might thus be said to describe, mathematically, the beginning of a vortical orientation within a vector space. (To designate "invariances in movement" I will use, depending on the context, the terms "form," "system," "object," "entity," or "consistency." I take the last term from Félix Guattari, who uses it to denote an entity that has a number of characteristics rather than the specific characteristic of an entity to "cohere." To denote the latter I will use "consistence".)

Mathematically, vectors in a vector space show those directions and orientations within a transformation that remain invariant, and they measure the scalar changes of those vectors, which are marked by stretching and compression. As vectors can represent different parameters, such as speed, magnetism, darkness, pressure, or spatial rotation, the operations of stretching and compression can in turn represent various forms of increase or decrease, such as that of the intensity of light or the speed of a movement. Eigenvectors and eigenvalues, then, might be said to script lines of force and intensity. Mathematically, the draining of Marion's blood in the famous shower-scene sequence in Hitchcock's movie *Psycho* can be described as a movement within the virtual multiplicity of vectors in a vector space. The vortex, as the axis of symmetry, is the eigenvector, while the speed of flow [*scaling*] measures the vortical system's eigenvalue. In a vectorial transformation, then, the eigenvector names the preserved direction, while the eigenvalue names the amount by which it has been scaled.

What if the movement of a vector within a vector space were to concern painting rather than mathematics? In the rotation and simultaneous stretching of a figure, the invariant axis of rotation would identify the eigenvector of the image while the amount by which it is stretched or compressed would identify its eigenvalue. In the context of the stretching and torsion of figures in mannerist painting, one might perhaps define the dynamics defined by eigenvectors and eigenvalues as a form of mathematical mannerism.

The vector space in which eigenvectors are defined might thus be described as a mathematical milieu or medium that contains an infinite number of virtual vectors from which specific vectors are actualized. Within such a vector space, the movements of a mathematical object are described as a set of vectorial changes, such as speed, direction, or expansion, in which one or more vectors remain invariant. In this context, eigenvectors may be said to extract a vectorial territory from a vectorial milieu. As such, the emergence of eigenvectors is the mathematical version of the physical process of the genesis of form, as in processes of crystallization, which also involve the emergence of a common orientation in a set of singular elements. In once more mathematical terms, eigenvalues create and delimit a mathematical "eigenspace" [*Eigenraum*], which describes the set of all eigenvectors of a transformation that have the same eigenvalue. The main reason why the term eigenvalue could migrate so easily from mathematics to other sciences is that it is possible to abstract its logic from vectorial to systemic change. If one assumes that eigenvalues and eigenvectors define invariants within systems while these undergo transformations—including those of their emergence and dissolution— they can also be used to model systems or entities in relation to the transformations that they undergo. Or, if one stresses the processual rather than the systemic side, eigenvalues and eigenvectors isolate entities within processes by defining invariants within these processes. If no eigenvector or eigenvalue can be identified in a specific process, that process is not *system*atic or *object*ive because it is impossible to identify an invariant element that could be said to have undergone the process. In other words, to identify an eigenvector or an eigenvalue is to define an "object in process" by way of its invariant characteristics within that process. In a world of constant metamorphosis, eigenvectors and eigenvalues identify a system's structural spine, what German sociologist Niklas Luhmann calls the "eigenaction of the system [*Eigentätigkeit des Systems*]" (*Gesellschaft1*, 67). Its "tenor," one might say, or its "refrain."

The minimal definition of a system, then, is "something that is undergoing change," and it is only within the parameters of that continuous change that a system can be defined *as* a system. Any system "x" is merely "the invariance in undergoing the transformational process y," with "y" being itself a complex term in the sense that a system tends to undergo not only one but a multiplicity of processes simultaneously.

Although an unsystemic white noise, as a state without eigenvalues, exists as a mathematical ideal, in the embodied world every process invariably contains eigenvectors and eigenvalues even if these might be imperceptible from certain plateaus of registration and observation. If the world is seen as an infinitely complex machinic system, the question about the presence of such eigenvectors and eigenvalues is both epistemological and ontological. As they might exist for only infinitesimally short durations or concern infinitesimally small scales, the ability to register them depends solely on the specific temporal and spatial scale of the apparatus of perception and observation, whether this is the human eye, an electron microscope, or the surfaces of sensation that fish use to perceive currents in a body of water or subtle changes in temperature. In other words, the world is everywhere infinitely processual and infinitely systemic, although in terms of perception, it is only finitely so. Living in the world means to align these infinite and finite mathematics.

On this conceptual background, a system is no longer "that which has a structural essense" but rather "a set of invariants within a larger processual milieu," or, from the systemic side, a set of invariant characteristics [*Eigenschaften*] within a series of constant transformation. Accordingly, the notion of substance is replaced by what is variously called subsistence, consistence, coherence, or structural integrity.

To show the insistence of the logic of eigenvalues in today's cultural and media studies contexts, let me turn to "eigenfaces," which form a subset of what are called "eigenimages" [*Eigenbilder*]. Eigenfaces are modeled on sets of invariants that define individual faces over longer periods of time, such as bone structure or the distance between the eyes, where "longer" is defined according to a human time-scale rather than the time-scale of a fruit-fly or a geological formation. They consist of sets of eigenvectors and eigenvalues that are derived from statistical analysis of many pictures of a particular face. They show their consistence, therefore, rather than their essence or stable substance. In the context of human face recognition and biometrics, eigenfaces mark the invariants that define individual faces within the multiplicity of processual flows that these faces undergo from moment to moment. In terms of biometric control, eigenfaces concern those facial characteristics that are difficult to artificially alter. In this context, face recognition "by eigenfaces" supplements other practices of identification by eigenvalues and eigenvectors, such as handwriting analysis, voice recognition, fingerprinting, or retinal recognition.

Abstract eigenfaces are not only part of overt practices of surveillance, however, they are also used in commercial, seemingly user-oriented face recognition programs. iPhoto's "Faces" application, for instance, identifies and selects individual faces from a photostream. If it finds enough instances of a specific face, it automatically collects photographs that contain that face in a specific folder. In order to identify faces, "Faces," like all face-recognition programs, uses algorithmic procedures that work on invariant physiological vectors that lie on a deeper structural level than a face's day-to-day changes.

Another use of the logic of eigenvalues is to show the connectivity of a node in a network, such as the connectivity of an individual's virtual persona in the social media. In order to model and measure that connectivity, the network is arranged according to "eigenvalue centrality," which means that nodes are arranged in a hierarchical relation to specific eigenvalue positions, with connections to high-scoring nodes—

nodes with a strong nodal eigenvalue, which is a value defined by the number of "habitual" settings up of a connection—contributing more to the score of the node in question than equal connections to low-scoring nodes. The more a node is connected to highly connected nodes, the stronger its eigenvalue centrality.

As the above examples show, the cultural context in which the identification of an entity's eigenvalues—that is, the identification of its various structural invariants—is particularly urgent today is cybernetic control and surveillance. As I write this, algorithms whose sole function is to identify eigenvalues and eigenvectors are trawling the internet. Each selfie that is caught in the net of these algorithms can be identified, selected, classified, and then stored in databanks, or used to track a person's movements. In that it underlies the increasing mathematization of control, the concept of eigenvalues is seminal in the implementation of practices of surveillance and thus in the creation of what Gilles Deleuze has called our contemporary "societies of control."

The identification of eigenvalues, however, extends beyond cultural practices of identification and collection to include virtually every "big data" application. Each form of quantitative research in fact rests on the identification of eigenvalues, from the identification of eigenfrequencies in the search for material faults in serially produced objects to Franco Moretti's attempt in *Distant Reading* to identify eigenvalues in works of art across specific periods of time or diverse genres. The notion of eigenvalue also informs many debates in academia, such as, currently, those concerning the field of new materialisms, where it can provide a useful conceptual tool to define both material and immaterial entities.

A final word of conceptual caution, however. Although eigenvalues and eigenvectors can be mathematically defined as sets of invariants within processes of transformation, the infinitely machinic nature of the embodied world makes true invariance impossible except as a conceptual ideal. On imperceptible temporal and spatial scales, every embodied system is defined by constant changes. On this background, even the gradual, imperceptibly minute expansion or contraction of metal at different temperatures counts as an immensely coarse change. Every seemingly invariant system, in fact, is defined by infinitely subtle changes. For the moment, however, and for purely pragmatic reasons, I will disregard the abstraction and idealization that is inherent in calling something "invariant." *Mathematically, systems are local and temporally stable "patterns in time and space," sets of eigenvalues moving within a constantly changing vectorial milieu or "media multiplicity."*

Chapter 2

PHYSICS: 1926

As John Aldrich notes about the shift of the term eigenvalue into physics, it was the development of Werner Heisenberg's matrix mechanics in the 1920s that "promoted the use of the eigen terminology, for the new theory," which as one of the first conceptualizations of a quantum logic, "was written in the language of Hilbert and his school" (n.p.). Apart from matrix mechanics, Erwin Schrödinger's alternative version of quantum theory promoted this shift. In both contexts, the notion of eigenvalues pertains to the complementarity of particle and wave, or, in Niels Bohr's terms, of "isolated material particle" and "radiation in free space" ("Quantum Postulate", 581).

Before I discuss the presence of eigenvalues in quantum physics, I should mention another set of *caveats*. The field of quantum mechanics is a fascinating but also a notoriously complicated and until today highly contested field. Inevitably, therefore, my account will contain numerous slippages and reductions. It will also disregard the historical complexity of the internal debates, such as Werner Heisenberg's revisions of his indeterminacy principle or Erwin Schrödinger's gradual shift away from quantum mechanics. Also, as I noted in the introduction, my account does not aim at being mathematical and in this respect cannot be "critical."

The core of my argument concerns the conceptual superposition of physics and philosophy, which, as can be seen in Werner Heisenberg's title *Physics and Philosophy*, is a topic that pervades quantum physics. In the light of the logic of quantum physics, in fact, one might talk not only of the meeting of physics and philosophy or the moment when physics "becomes" philosophy and vice versa, but rather of the "collapse" of an indeterminate or indifferent conceptual field into the fields of physics and philosophy respectively. Specifically, I will address the question how, from within the logic of eigenvalues, the scientific notion of complementarity reconfigures the relation between the ontic, the ontological, and the epistemological.

In many ways, my reading relies on accounts of quantum physics that are aimed at a general readership. These texts, in particular Karen Barad's *Meeting the Universe Halfway: Quantum Physics and the Entanglement of Matter and Meaning* and the work of Arkady Plotnitsky, form the conceptual cloud around the nucleus of this chapter, which consists of close readings of a number of passages from the work of Erwin Schrödinger.

The most obvious and fundamental moment of the presence of the notion of eigenvalues in quantum physics concerns a paper that is often considered to mark the very origin of quantum physics, Schrödinger's "Quantisierung als Eigenwertproblem" (*Annalen*, 109) from 1926, translated as "Quantisation as a Problem of Proper Values." (I should perhaps note that in this title, "quantisation" refers to the shift from classical physics to quantum theory rather than to acts of counting or measuring, which would be referred to as "quantification").

Before I get to that paper, some words about the translation of that title and more generally about the history of the translation of the term eigenvalue into English, which often obscures the term's history. As John Aldrich notes, "[i]n 1926 P. A. M. Dirac was writing 'a set of independent solutions which may be called eigenfunctions' ('On the Theory of Quantum Mechanics') [. . .] *Eigenvalue* appears in a letter to *Nature* [. . .] from A. S. Eddington [. . .] *Eigenvector* appears in R. Brauer & H. Weyl's 'Spinors in *n* Dimensions'" (in Miller, n.p.). Concurrently, the term was translated as "proper value," which "has been a standard English rendering of 'eigen' – thus in the nineteenth century, Helmholtz's *Eigentöne* became 'proper tones'" (Aldrich in Miller, n.p.). In Aldrich's account, the debate about the terminology was decided in the 1970s in favor of eigenvalues (in Miller, n.p.). If one disregards that history, it is difficult to realize that, as it does in Schrödinger's paper, "proper value" equals "eigenvalue."

Schrödinger's paper introduces what has since come to be known as the "Schrödinger equation," which functionalizes the problem of measuring the position of an electron within a phase space in order to be able to predict that particle's future position; in quantum theoretical terms, to be able to chart its time-evolution or, in other words, to measure the "probability density" or "particle configuration" at a specific position or moment.

These terms—not "position," but "probability density," not particle, but "particle configuration"—already indicate the novelty of Schrödinger's approach, which is to consider an electron, and thus what is commonly considered to be a particle, from within the theoretical parameters of a wave equation (ψ-function).

Schrödinger notes that he was "led to these deliberations in the first place by the suggestive papers of of Louis de Broglie" ("Quantisation," 9), who, in his 1924 dissertation *Recherches sur la théorie des Quanta*, was the first to use a wave equation to describe particles and to postulate that not only light, but matter in general was defined by what he called the "wave-particle duality." In particular, Schrödinger was interested in de Broglie's thoughts about the "space distribution" of what de Broglie called "phase waves" (9). As Heisenberg notes, "Schrödinger tried to set up a wave equation for de Broglie's stationary waves around the nucleus. Early in 1926 he succeeded in deriving the energy values of the stationary states of the hydrogen atom as 'Eigenvalues' of his wave equation" (41).

Although Schrödinger relies on de Broglie, he takes his ideas in a different direction. "The main difference is that de Broglie thinks of progressive waves, while we are led to stationary proper vibrations [*Eigenschwingungen*] if we interpret our formulae as representing vibrations. I have lately shown that the Einstein gas theory can be based on the consideration of such stationary proper vibrations [*stehender Eigenschwingungen*], to which the dispersion law of de Broglie's phase waves has been applied" ("Quantisation," 9).

Schrödinger's intuition is that the "quantum jumps" of electrons that orbit the nucleus of an atom can be understood much more elegantly and adequately in terms of wave-like behavior; more specifically, in terms of what he calls "proper vibration processes" "*Eigenschwingungsvorgänge*" (9). One advantage of looking at the energy distribution of electrons in terms of a "standing wave"—rather than as particles and de Broglie's notion of a "progressive wave"—is that changes in their discrete energy levels, which Bohr's traditional model illustrates by way of different orbits around the atomic nucleus, can be understood, mathematically, no longer as the discrete jumps of particles between fixed orbits, but as the modulations of the eigenfrequency of a standing wave that pervades, at each moment, the energetic space around the nucleus. As Schrödinger notes, "[i]t is hardly necessary to emphasize how much more congenial it would be to imagine that at a quantum transition the energy changes over from one form of vibration to another, than to think of a jumping electron. The changing of the vibration form can take place *continuously* in space and time" (11, emphasis added).

In Schrödinger's treatment, then, an electron is understood in terms of "a standing wave" with a specific eigenfrequency and an eigenstate [*Eigenzustand*]. (In terms of translation, the term eigenstate is interesting in that "[w]hile eigenvalue, eigenfunction and eigenvector were translations of German originals, the *eigenstate* of Dirac's *Principles of Quantum Mechanics* (1930, 35) was a new construction and it marks the arrival of *eigen* as a fully English particle. *Eigenstate* was translated into German as *Eigenzustand*" (Aldrich, n.p.).)

The term eigenstate designates the state that is associated with a definite value of an object or particle and is considered as analogous to a discrete energy level of the system in ψ (*Eigenfunktion*). As Bohr notes, "[i]ndeed, the proper vibrations [*Eigenschwingungen*] of the Schrödinger wave equation have been found to furnish a representation of the stationary states of an atom meeting all requirements. The energy of each state is connected with the corresponding period of vibration according to the general quantum relation" ("Quantum Postulate," 586). Because of the conceptual diffraction of electrons into both particle- and wave-like behavior, in terms of eigenvalues, the "variation problem has a discrete and a continuous spectrum of proper values [*Eigenwertspektrum*]" (Schrödinger, "Quantisation," 2).

In terms of classical physics, particles showing wave-like behavior and vice versa presents a dilemma, because it considers particles and waves as fundamentally different. In terms of eigenvalues, isolated material particles have individual eigenstates that are associated with particular characteristics such as color or spin value. In my earlier example from *Psycho*, for instance, spin is "a vector quantity" (Barad, *Meeting the Universe Halfway*, 258), with the direction of an arrow that represents the eigenvector marking the "spin axis" (258) and the length of the arrow the speed of the rotation. When they form groups, particles retain these characteristics. In other words, collections of particles form mixtures.

Although waves have eigenfunctions and eigenstates as well, such as the eigenfrequency of an individual sound- or light-wave, groups of waves form superpositions [*Überlagerungen*] rather than mixtures, which is the property that allows for processes of interference and diffraction. The difference might be illustrated by jumping into a pool filled with plastic balls and jumping into a pool filled with water, or of hearing a set of single notes and of hearing a chord.

In terms of eigenvalues, in mixtures, particles retain their individual, discrete eigenstates, while in superpositions, single waves create communal, continuous interference patterns without individual eigenstates. Like drops of water in the ocean, individual eigenstates dissolve into what might be called an overall, communal eigenstate. Perhaps, however, it would be more precise to talk of a superposition as having an indifferent or virtual eigenstate that is actualized into a differentiated eigenstate by its measurement.

If "indifferent" is understood mathematically as "not yet differentiated" rather than ethically as "not caring," differentiation translates a multiplicity of indifferent movements into differentiated, measured or integrated vectors, the question being about the "adequation" of difference to indifference. Similarly, if one defines quantity as "that which is unqualified" rather than as a particular amount of something, one might say that the measurement qualifies a quantitative eigenstate.

Gilles Deleuze's philosophical differentiation into intensive, virtual difference and extensive, actual difference sets up a similar logic. "Difference in itself" is "that intensity in itself as the original moment at which it is neither qualified nor extended" (*Difference*, 237). This "[d]ifference in the form of intensity remains implicated in itself, while it is cancelled by being explicated in extensity" (228). Similarly, in terms of mathematics, "[e]very number is originally intensive and vectorial in so far as it implies a difference of quantity which cannot properly be cancelled" (232). When it is not used "in quotation," I will take "energy" to refer to actual, extended intensity and "intensity" to refer to virtual energy. Energy is "intensity in a state of extensity" or "qualified intensity."

Although a pattern of superposed waves can be broken down into single waves by way of a Fourier analysis, a fundamental difference between mixtures and superpositions is, as Schrödinger emphasizes, that "[w]hen two systems interact, their ψ-functions [...] do not come into interaction but rather they immediately *cease to exist and a single one, for the combined system takes their place*" ("Present Situation," 167, emphasis added). Even more surprisingly, "[a]s soon as the systems begin to influence each other, the combined function ceases to be a product and moreover does not again divide up, after they have again become separated, into factors that can be assigned individually to the systems" (167).

Let me disregard what a bewildered Albert Einstein called "spooky-action-at-a-distance" (Barad, *Meeting the Universe Halfway*, 315)—the fact that having once interacted "as waves," two particles remain mysteriously linked even when they have moved apart—and remain with the less spooky but perhaps equally disturbing characteristic that, in a quantum state, particles act like waves and vice versa, which boils down, in physics, to the question of how to deal with experiments that show "[a] superposition or interference pattern made by particles" (269) and waves acting "as" particles. As these experiments register what according to classical physics are incompatible and even contradictory behaviors, it is no longer possible to posit a categorical difference between particle and wave. Or, more precisely, although it is still possible to "meaningfully speak of 'wave' and 'particle' characteristics" (298), one can do so "only within their respective limits" (298) and one has to treat these limits as "*inversely related* to one another" (298, emphasis added). To say that particle and wave are complementary means, somewhat paradoxically, that the two states are conceptually opposed but that this conceptual opposition is somehow suspended in a quantum state. This suspension, in fact, is what literally "makes up" the quantum state as a state characterized by the "double exposure" of oppositional, inversely related characteristics.

What does this blurring of the classical categories mean in terms of eigenvalues? How to visualize a state of complementarity? And what does the notion of measurement have to do with what is called the "collapse of complementarity?" All of these are questions Schrödinger addresses in his paper "The Present Situation in Quantum Mechanics."

In classical mechanics, one can provide a sharp measurement [*scharfe Messung*] that allows one to predict both the position and the momentum of an electron. In Schrödinger's equation, this is no longer possible. In his terminology, while the "expectation-catalog" (159) about a particle can be fully known in classical physics, under quantum conditions, only half of that catalog can be known at any one time. Schrödinger calls this the "disjunctive splitting of the expectation-catalog" (162). While Heisenberg's uncertainty principle [*Unschärferelation*] is based on the inevitable intervention of the measuring device into what is measured, with the precision of the measurement of a particle's position inversely related to the precision of the measurement of its momentum or impulse, for Schrödinger it has to do with the particle-wave duality, which no longer allows a particle to be treated as a particle. "The classical concept of *state* becomes lost, in that at most a well-chosen *half* of a complete set of variables can be assigned definite numerical values [...] The other half then remains completely indeterminate" (153). Although for different reasons than for Heisenberg, more knowledge about position entails less knowledge about momentum and vice versa.

Is it possible to illustrate the quantum logic from within the logic of the ψ-function? Can one make that logic, as Schrödinger calls it, vivid [*anschaulich*]? What if one were to apply the quantum logic to some well-known, everyday phenomenon? Say the particle was a cat. Let's put that cat into a "black box:" "A cat is penned up in a steel chamber, along with the following device (which must be secured against direct interference by the cat): in a Geiger counter there is a tiny bit of radioactive substance, *so* small, that *perhaps* in the course of the hour one of the atoms decays, but also, with equal probability, perhaps none; if it happens, the counter tube discharges and through a relay releases a hammer which shatters a small flask of hydrocyanic acid. If one has left this entire system to itself for an hour, one would say that the cat still lives *if* meanwhile no atom has decayed. The ψ-function of the entire system would express this by having in it the living and dead cat (pardon the expression) mixed [*gemischt*] or smeared out [*verschmiert*] in equal parts" (157).

Schrödinger's telescoping of the quantum state from the microscopic to the macroscopic level—where, as we know today, quantum states can also be observed—illustrates the weird idea that on extremely small scales, entities such as electrons or photons show the behavior of both particle and wave by way of the even weirder idea that during the time that the cat is unobserved, it is in an indeterminate state in relation to being dead or alive.

This indeterminacy does not imply that the cat has an equal chance of being alive or dead, or that it is both dead and alive at the same time. Rather, and this is where the notion of eigenstates becomes crucial, it means that while it is unobserved in the chamber, which illustrates in terms of a real space the conceptual space of the ψ-function, the cat does not have an individual eigenstate—neither that of being dead nor that of being alive—because "it," which means the "system of the cat," is dissolved in the general indeterminacy operative in the chamber; in the state of the superposition of eigenstates, that is.

The weirdness of the image, of course, lies in how it clashes with our intuitive experience and conceptualization of reality. Already in "Quantisation as a Problem of Proper Values," Schrödinger had noted differences between model and reality. For instance, "the idea of only *one* proper vibration [*Eigenschwingung*] being excited whenever the atom does not radiate—if we must hold fast to this idea—is very far removed from the *natural* picture of a vibrating system. We know that a macroscopic system does not behave like that, but yields in general a potpourri of its proper vibrations [*Eigenschwingungen*]" (11). While that difference concerned merely the model's inherent idealizations, however, in the case of the cat, "serious misgivings arise if one notices that the uncertainty affects macroscopically tangible and visible things, for which the term 'blurring' seems simply wrong" ("Present Situation," 156). Schrödinger himself, in fact, calls the image of a "blurred cat" "ridiculous [*burlesk*]" (157), which might be why Heisenberg, in *Physics and Philosophy*, uses the less drastic example of an atom in a chamber rather than a cat (157–160).

As Schrödinger had noted, from within the conceptual given of superposition, before the box is opened in order to see which of the cat's eigenstates has actualized itself, the cat's superposed eigenstates should be imagined as being equally "mixed" [*gemischt*] or "smeared" [*verschmiert*] across the inside of the chamber. Although this image might help to get an idea of the particle–wave duality, it is still highly counter-intuitive. Even for the time that we cannot see the cat, we tend to think of it as either alive or dead. For Schrödinger, however, it is only, and quite literally, the moment of what he variously calls measurement, observation, or "inspection" ("Present Situation," 162), that decides which of the two eigenstates of the system is in actual fact [*eigentlich*] true. In terms of eigenstates, while the state of the cat before the observation is defined by "a superposition of eigenstates" (Barad, *Meeting the Universe Halfway*, 280), at the moment of observation we find the cat "in *one* of the possible eigenstates" (280).

The notion of eigenstates is what allows one to make sense of Schrödinger's conceit. On a microscopic level, before a specific "particle's" position or impulse is measured, "it" forms part of a communal superposition of eigenstates. As I noted, the reason why "its" "position" and "momentum" can only be probabilistic is not, as in Heisenberg's theory, that the measuring device intervenes in the measurement, but that "it" is conceptually smeared across the phase space and thus can be at any position within that given space. I have put the terms particle, position, momentum, and "it" into quotation marks in the preceding sentence because in an unobserved state these "particular" parameters do in actual fact not exist or apply, as the ψ-function describes superpositions rather than mixtures. As "part of that equation," and at the "time of that equation," "they"—the particle and the cat respectively—are not in and they do not have a discrete eigenstate [*Eigenzustand*].

The continuous, potential state of "individual statelessness" "they" are in also helps to understand why classical causality can be put out of operation without having to give up a quantum-state, probabilistic causality. As Schrödinger notes, "[i]f a classical state does not exist at any moment, it can hardly change causally. What do change are the *statistics* or *probabilities*, *these* moreover causally" ("Present Situation," 154). After all, we are still doing science.

The measurement, then, "*resolves the indeterminacy*" (280). In Schrödinger's terms, the "eigenstate of the superposition"—the ψ-function, that is—is "collapsed" in the sense that it is reduced to an individual eigenstate, or, more precisely, to one eigenvalue. As Bergmann and Schaeffer note, "[t]he reduction of the eigenstate [...] into an eigenvalue [...] of the eigenstate is also called collapse of the eigenstate [...] or of the wave function" (63). In other words, at the time of measurement, the logic of superpositions "collapses" into the logic of mixtures.

What parameters are involved in this collapse? First, Schrödinger's intention is not to come to conclusions about the state of reality in and of itself. Second, the measurement does not "in reality" turn waves into particles. Rather, the collapse is only about the quantum-state's relation to the acts of measurement and modelization. It is exactly at this point in his argument that Schrödinger superposes physics and philosophy. As the question is less about a physics of reality than about a physics of measurement, he takes "recourse to epistemology" ("Present Situation," 157). Programmatically, the part of his paper where he talks about this relation is headlined "The Deliberate About-face of the Epistemological Viewpoint" [*Der bewußte Wechsel des epistemologischen Standpunkts*] (157).

Schrödinger is a superb stylist and an extremely careful writer. When he notes that "reality resists *imitation* through a model" (157, emphasis added), this is not a statement about reality, nor does it call for a critique of modelization as such. Rather, it calls for a critique of the naïve realism that is inherent in the logic of imitation, and as such about the realist assumption of classical physics that there is a state of reality that can be imitated by a model. This assumption is in turn based on the belief that an objective reality exists even when nobody is observing it, and that science can provide a correct model of that reality. Schrödinger, Bohr, and Heisenberg—at least according to Heisenberg's *Physics and Philosophy*, which can be read as a long meditation on the relation between physics and language—equally stake the logic of quantum physics against such a naïve realism. As Bohr notes, "the idea of complementarity is suited to characterise the situation, which bears a deep-going analogy to the general difficulty in the formation of human ideas, inherent in the distinction between subject and object" ("Quantum Postulate," 590)—between scientist and reality, that is.

Schrödinger's critique of a naïve realism plays itself out in the relation between reality, the ψ-function, and the collapse of the ψ-function. The "abrupt change by measurement" ("Present Situation," 158), Schrödinger maintains, is indeed "the most interesting point of the entire theory. It is precisely *the* point that demands the break with naive realism" (158). The genius of Schrödinger's move lies in positioning the "formalism of the ψ-function" *between* reality and model. "For *this* reason one can *not* put the ψ-function directly in place of the model or of the physical thing. And indeed not because one might never dare impute abrupt unforeseen changes to a physical thing [*Realding*] or to a model, but because in the realism point of view observation is a natural process like any other and cannot *per se* bring about an interruption of the orderly flow of natural events" (158). In quantum physics, however, it *can* and it *does*. While the measurement does not "in reality" turn waves into particles, it cuts into a continuous reality of which this discrete measurement is, at the same time, a part. Accordingly, the scientist is both "a part of" and "apart from" that continuous reality. In this context, Heisenberg will note that "the transition from the 'possible' to the 'actual' takes place during the act of observation" when there is an "interaction of the object with the measuring device" (*Physics and Philosophy*, 54). In this process, "[t]he observation itself changes the probability function discontinuously; it selects of all possible events the actual one that has taken place" (54).

It would be too easy, therefore, to maintain that the ψ-function is related to ontology, while its collapse is related to epistemology. Rather, the problem concerns three variables, with the ψ-function occupying a space between the ontic and the epistemological. It represents a state of "standing in the middle between the idea of an event and the actual event, a strange kind of physical reality just in the middle between possibility and reality" (42).

How does Schrödinger conceptualize the quantum-mechanical relation between these three registers? The measurement implies the "annihilation" [*Vernichtung*] ("Present Situation," 162) of the indeterminate quantum state—what he called the "disjunctive splitting of the expectation-catalog"—in that it "determines [*entscheidet*] the disjunction" (162). This qualitative jump, however, is not part *of* the measured object's ψ-function and it has no effect *on* that ψ-function, because already at the moment of observation, that function is "collapsed." "For it had disappeared, it was no more" (162).

Why? Where has it gone? The original, unobserved ψ-function "has become snarled up [*verheddert*], in accord with the causal law of the *combined* ψ-function, with that of the measuring instrument [*Verquickung*]" (161). I have already mentioned that the reason for this is that "as soon as the systems begin to influence each other, the combined function ceases to be a product." To illustrate that the cat's indeterminate state in the ψ-function has become entangled with the measuring device, Schrödinger uses the image of a map. "*The expectation-catalog of the object has split into a conditional disjunction of expectation-catalogs*—like a Baedeker that one has taken apart [*kunstgerecht zerlegt*] in the proper manner." (161–162).

In the operation of observation, the ψ-function "is born anew, is reconstituted, is separated out [*herausgelöst*] from the entangled knowledge that one has, through an act of perception" (162). In logical terms, the ψ-function's entanglement with the measuring device makes for its annihilation, in the same way in which in terms of chronology, the ψ-function has changed continuously between two measurements but discontinuously when it is measured. This fact is responsible for the non-causal character of the relation between any two measurements. Here as well, one can no longer talk of the "same" ψ-function. "From the form in which the ψ-function was last known, to the new in which it reappears, runs *no continuous* [*stetige*] *road*—it ran indeed through annihilation. Contrasting the two forms, the thing looks like a leap. In truth something of importance happens in between, namely the influence of the two bodies on each other, during which the object possessed no private expectation-catalog nor had any claim thereunto, because *it was not independent*" (162, emphases added).

Indeterminacy [*Unschärfe*], therefore, only pertains to the time "*between* measurements, and does not seem to describe *the abrupt transition that appears to take place as a result of the measurement*" (Barad, *Meeting the Universe Halfway*, 281). As Heisenberg will describe it from within an Aristotelian logic, "[i]f we want to describe what happens in an atomic event, we have to realize that the word 'happens' can apply only to the observation, not to the state of affairs between two observations" (54).

In terms of the logic of eigenvalues, Schrödinger's tale of the cat illustrates [*veranschaulicht*] that it is only after eigenstates and eigenvalues have been "actualized" through their measurement—a process that introduces a discontinuity into a continuous process and thus literally freezes them both spatially and temporally—that they can be said to "have" discrete states and values. In fact, Schrödinger maintains quite categorically that there simply *are* no values before the measurement, irrespective of whether these are "eigen" or not. If "a variable *has* no definite value before I measure it; then measuring it does not mean ascertaining a value that it *has*" ("Present Situation," 158). As "reality does not determine the measured value" (158), it is only the repetition of the measurement that allows one to determine the accuracy of the measurement. The truth is only ever probabilistic.

Is it the technical device that, when it performs the measurement, causes the collapse of the state of indeterminacy? Does the measuring device make the distinction that introduces a discontinuity into a continuous process? Predictably, the answer is both "yes" and "no." "Yes" because all measuring devices—from cells to oscilloscopes—introduce cuts into continua, or, in other words, qualities into quantities. When Schrödinger states that this is the reason why "[t]he discontinuity of the expectation catalog due to measurement is *unavoidable*" (160), this implies that all living entities consist of and quite literally are complex measuring machines. Difference engines. As Schrödinger notes in "Indeterminism and Free Will," "[w]e *must* decide. One thing *must* happen, *will* happen, life goes on. There is no ψ-function in life" (13).

This programmatic statement, of course, opens up the question of "what is life?," which is also the title and topic of one of Schrödinger's books. Here, it implies that one characteristic of individuated life is the "making of differences." Whatever "life" might be, Schrödinger argues, there is no individuated life without differentiation. As an assemblage of "differentiating entities"—what I will later refer to in terms of Félix Guattari as the "Plane of Consistencies"—mathematically speaking, the world is a complex assemblage of eigenvalues.

The answer is also "no," however, because for Schrödinger, the relevant measurement does not take place within trivial technical measuring machines. Rather, the complementarity collapses when a non-trivial, "living subject" ("Present Situation," 162) observes the result of the measurement. "[N]ot until this inspection, which determines the disjunction, does anything discontinuous, or leaping, take place. One is inclined to call this a *mental* action" (162). The technical machine merely registers. It does not measure in the sense that it "perceives" the registration. As perception equals measurement in that it cuts into continua, a true measurement must be "perceived."

Schrödinger describes the vicissitudes of measuring when, after his description of the state of the cat, he differentiates between a "shaky or out-of-focus photograph" and "a photograph of clouds and fog." "It is typical of these cases that an indeterminacy originally restricted to the atomic domain becomes transformed into macroscopic indeterminacy, which can then be *resolved* by direct observation. That prevents us from so naively accepting as valid a 'blurred [*verwaschenes*] model' for representing reality. In itself it would not embody [*enthalten*] anything unclear or contradictory. There is a difference between a shaky or out-of-focus photograph [*Photographie*] and a snapshot [*Aufnahme*] of clouds and fog banks" (157).

A little earlier in the paper Schrödinger had noted that "it is in fact not impossible to express the degree and kind of blurring of *all* variables in *one* perfectly clear concept" (156). The tool for this is the "wave function or ψ-function" (156) as an "imagined entity [*Gedankending*, literally 'a thing of thought'] that images the blurring of all variables at every moment just as clearly and faithfully as the classical model does its sharp numerical values" (156, my brackets). Again, one might map this onto Deleuze's mathematical differentiation of extensive and intensive numbers: "The vectors or vectorial magnitudes which occur throughout extensity, but also the scalar magnitudes or particular cases of vector-potentials, are the eternal *witness to* the intensive origin" (*Difference and Repetition*, 231, emphasis added). Somewhat paradoxically, the act of quantification consists of a qualification that should be adequate *to* rather than the representation *of* a given intensity.

In terms of Schrödinger's example, a snapshot of clouds and fog provides a clear model of a blurred reality. Both clouds and fog show wave-like behavior, so that a snapshot of this state shows, very clearly and accurately, a wave-like "state without distinction." The ψ-function, which also does not contain distinctions "before" or "without" a measurement, is analogous to such a blurred landscape. The last part of the sentence can thus be read as: the snapshot-like measurement provides a clear and distinct image—a "portrait" or "simulacrum" [*Abbild*]—of an obscure and indistinct [*verwaschene*] world, or, in Schrödinger's terms, of reality. In principle, therefore, quantum mechanics creates a distinct image of an indistinct, obscure world, an image that is, in itself, neither "unclear" [*unklar*] nor contradictory [*widerspruchsvoll*].

As the ψ-function is entangled with the measuring device, at the "unavoidable" moment of measurement, the obscurity of the world without distinctions is collapsed into and trailed by the clear model of the world with distinctions. The measurement turns the indistinct ψ-function into a distinct snapshot. Through all of this, of course, the world remains ontically "as it is."

The ψ-function and its collapse together provide a clear and distinct image of an obscure and indistinct state that it trails behind, in the same way that the snapshot of a blurred reality cannot simply subtract the clouds and fog banks from the image in order to make that image distinct and clear. It is in reference to such a notion of a sharp snapshot of a blurred reality, as opposed to the naïve belief in a clear, numerical reality, that the quantum model is a blurred model. It is as such that it lies in-between the ontic and the epistemological. Before "its" measurement, it describes reality as indistinct [*unscharf*]. As collapsed, however, it describes reality as distinct [*scharf*]. The new epistemology, then, rests on a distinct model—the collapsed ψ-function—that trails an indistinct reality behind.

As such, it can never reach a reality that is considered as something with which measuring entities are not entangled. It can, however, be adequate to an indistinct reality that is defined by the unobserved ψ-function, which it collapses. As the model can never be based on the assumption of it allowing for a clear representation of reality, it contains, in itself, the inevitable, built-in obscurity of the blurred world. Its clarity is the clarity of obscurity, its distinctness the distinctness of the indistinct. Its measurements actualize one specific eigenvalue from a field of potentiality. Dead or alive. Either, or. Every measurement trails an unmeasured, indistinct state of superposition behind as a given state with which it is inevitably entangled.

Again, one must admire Schrödinger's choice of words and metaphors. By way of the in-between position of the ψ-function, the indeterminacy [*Unschärfe*] of the world has traveled from the ontic level (physical reality) to the ontological (the ψ-function) and further to the epistemological level (the collapsed ψ-function). It has moved from reality to model, which in Schrödinger's description literally contains, by way of the word "blurred," quantum physics' uncertainty relation [*Unschärferelation*].

To represent a blurred world, the epistemological model has to remain "in itself"—inherently, that is—tied to that blurred world. As such, it can no longer provide a transparent imitation of a "sharp reality." Like Bohr, Schrödinger maintains that both language and conceptualization are based on differentiation, and as such are involved in the problematics of quantum physics. Bohr insists, in fact, that already the terms particle and wave are "abstractions" ("Quantum Postulate," 586) and as such different from physical reality, which is conceptualized, in language, as continuous, but which is "in actual fact" only "what it is." All one can do, therefore, is to provide a model that incorporates the characteristic of "determination of the indeterminate", a model that models its own entanglement in the indifferent that it differentiates.

While Schrödinger relates differentiation to a human observer, that field has been extended "after Schrödinger." What, for instance, if the world were to be conceptualized as everywhere and at all times "making distinctions?" This is the direction John Bell takes when he expands the logic that Schrödinger addresses to human cognition and mentality, to reality as such. "If the theory is to apply to anything but highly idealized laboratory operations, are we not obliged to admit that more or less 'measurement-like' processes are going on more or less all the time, more or less everywhere?" (216). Such a world would consist of an infinity of both conscious and unconscious measurements, as well as human and non-human observation and cognition. In fact, according to the mathematical logic of the Dedekind cut, "at infinity" the indistinct, superposed universe is "identical to" the distinct, collapsed universe.

Although the debates between Heisenberg, Schrödinger, and Bohr are themselves immensely entangled, one can identify, roughly, three aspects of indeterminacy [*Unschärfe*]. For Heisenberg, the reason for indeterminacy in measurements of very small systems lies in the impossibility of the apparatus of observation to physically not disturb, and thus not to interfere with the state of the observed. Schrödinger is less concerned with the mechanics of the measuring device than with the general logic and the vicissitudes of measurement. These result from the fact that the eigenstate of the cat as alive and the opposite eigenstate of the cat as dead are ontically entangled [*verschränkt*] with the eigenstate of the atom as either decayed or not decayed, with the additional entanglement of the cat with the apparatus of observation and the observer and the resulting antinomies of entanglement. As Barad notes, "the fate of the cat is entangled with the fate of the atom, and in the absence of an appropriate measuring apparatus, their fates are indeterminate" (*Meeting the Universe Halfway*, 278). The eigenstate of a particle is entangled with a wave function.

Still, although the distinction into a discrete eigenstate and eigenvalue is brought about by an act of perception, to note, as Barad does, that Schrödinger's notion of complementarity is "*explicitly epistemic, not ontic*" (284) is perhaps too restricted. Schrödinger's *Gedankenexperiment* is epistemological in terms of the observer's collapse of the ψ-function. In that the observer's perceptual cuts are introduced into a reality that is, from within an analog logic of waves, conceptualized as unobserved, however, the experiment is not restricted to the epistemological. In fact, any reduction of the overall problematics to an, albeit unavoidable "collapse" of the entanglements of the ontic, the ontological and the epistemological into separate fields might be inadequate to the complexity of the logic of quantum mechanics.

In his paper "On the Notions of Causality and Complementarity," Bohr, who Barad singles out as the one scientist who claims that reality itself is complementary, defines the ψ-function as a mathematical means, stressing in particular its non-pictorial and thus anti-representational dimensions: "The entire formalism is to be considered as a tool for deriving predictions, of definite or statistical character, as regards information obtainable under experimental conditions described in classical terms and specified by means of parameters entering into the algebraic or differential equations of which the matrices or the wave functions, respectively, are solutions. These symbols themselves, as is indicated already by the use of imaginary numbers, are not susceptible to pictorial interpretation; and even derived real functions like densities and currents are only to be regarded as expressing the probabilities for the occurrence of individual events observable under well-defined experimental conditions" (314). The quantum argument has to navigate between the Skylla of a naïve realism that assumes a reality "out there" that models can imitate, and the Charybdis of assuming that reality is in actual fact produced by measurements. Rather, what entanglement means is that measurements, as a mode of differentiation, are part of science and of living. They are part and parcel of individually lived reality, of the world considered as a multiplicity of eigenlives and eigenworlds.

This state follows a logic in which phenomena are treated, in the words of Gilles Deleuze, as "*formally distinct*, while being ontologically identical" (*Expressionism*, 64, emphasis added). As no two things, whether objects or thoughts, are ever identical, the term should here be understood in the sense of "indistinct." (In terms of science, I will use "formal" to refer to the measured and differentiated world, in terms of media studies, to "form" as opposed to "medium.")

Somewhat counter-intuitively, the notions of entanglement and complementarity are precisely why science cannot claim that reality is entangled or complementary. While the scientist is part of and entangled in the purely quantitative, "superposed world," any model of that entanglement must include that world's qualification by way of a measurement, or, to stress the passage from quantity to quality, by way of the evaluation that collapses the ψ-function. To ignore this inevitable collapse would reinstate, although with a number of *caveats*, a naïve logic of imitation that puts too much trust in metaphors and models, precisely the trust quantum physics had originally set out to replace by way of the formalism of a "blurred model."

Quantum physics' claim is not to propose a truth about the ontic considered as the given reality. Its more modest claim is to propose a coherent ontology and epistemology. Certain experiments have caused science to consider a new model of reality that uses the terms "entanglement" and "complementarity" to conceptualize that reality, although it knows that these are, like the terms "particle" and "wave," abstractions. What science does is to shift from a naïve epistemology to what might be called, in reference back to Schrödinger, a "collapsed epistemology" that trails the blurred, indifferent, and unobserved ontic world behind.

If quantum theory argues that all one can say about the ontic state of reality is that it is "as it is," this statement is neither something that has been proven, nor something that is assumed as a conceptual *a priori*. Rather, it is the result of scientific experiments and measurements that prove only that the naïve realism of classical physics, which had assumed that reality and its measurement were not entangled, has run into inconsistencies. It is this realization rather than discoveries about how reality "in actual fact" functions, that causes the specific quantum ontology and the quantum epistemology.

On this background, quantum physics is more about logic and science—as Heisenberg notes, it is about the fact that one can, even in science, no longer use classical logic: "In quantum theory this law 'tertium non datur' is to be modified" (156)—than a claim about the ontic world. Heisenberg, Schrödinger, and Bohr would agree that, as Heisenberg notes, "what we observe is not nature in itself but nature exposed to our method of questioning" (57). At the same time, they would also agree that "the system which is treated by the methods of quantum mechanics is in fact a part of a much bigger system (eventually the whole world); it is interacting with this bigger system [...] of which the observer is a part" (153).

Can one say if, and how far, the logic of entanglement reaches into reality? For Barad, what Bohr calls the "phenomenon" denotes "physical reality" (274) under the condition that it includes "the entire [...] entangled experimental arrangement" (*Meeting the Universe Halfway*, 275). The difference between classical physics and quantum theory lies in that the latter's "objective referent[s] of measured properties" (309) are phenomena rather than "observation-independent object[s]" (275) considered from the condition of an "immediate givenness" (244) of the world. To addresses the epistemological question, Barad takes recourse to topology: "how can we account for the fact that measurements produce determinate values?" (344). A scientific, empirical epistemology is encapsulated within an overall entangled reality. "Objectivity is a matter of exteriority-within-the-phenomenon" (346).

In the debate about where exactly the claim about the entanglement and complementarity of reality cuts into the superposed fields of the ontic, the ontological, and the epistemological, Arkady Plotnitsky comes down squarely on the epistemological side. "A crucial point of Bohr's phenomenon is that it precludes any description or even conception of quantum objects themselves and their behavior. Which behavior is, nevertheless, responsible for the emergence of these phenomena and the effects defining each such quality" (*Niels Bohr and Complementarity*, 141). The fundamental "[d]ifference between quantum *objects* and observed *phenomena*" (147) needs to be preserved. Arguing from a new-materialist perspective, Barad's argument leans toward the ontic side. "*Complementarity is an ontic (not merely an epistemic) principle*" (*Meeting the Universe Halfway*, 309), she notes. In her recent work, Barad develops this argument further toward a comprehensive notion of fields as "patterns of energy" ("Transmaterialities," 395) and of measurements in which "there is no collapse" (422) and thus no creation of "particularities" with specific eigenvalues.

How to mediate between these contesting approaches? As entangled, the observer is always in a state of immanence considered as a state in which ontic, ontological, and epistemological levels are themselves considered as complementary domains. Formally, however, an ontic perspective "excludes" ontology and epistemology in the same way that, inversely, the ontic given—in quantum mechanics: the world, physical reality, or the quantum object—is "excluded" in ontology and epistemology.

Let me address this apparent antinomy by way of a superposition of quantum theory and philosophy. In a lecture during the summer semester of 1927, Martin Heidegger used, for the first time, the difference between "Being" [*Sein*] and "beings" [*Seiendes*]. While Being denotes physical reality in its givenness as "factical existence [*faktische Existenz*]" (*Being and Time* [BT], 299; *Sein und Zeit* [SZ], 325)., the level of "beings" [*Seiendes*] concerns embodied reality as the way in which the given is given.

Heidegger's work, which shows a close, although sometimes critical conceptual relation to quantum theory—in particular to Heisenberg, with whom he exchanged three letters in 1953—provides a useful figure of thought to help resolve or at least to enframe the debate between the two extreme positions. For Heidegger, the "ontic" concerns Being, while the "ontological" concerns the philosophical analysis of Being [*Untersuchung des Seins*].

As in quantum physics, these levels are entangled in that "Being is always the being of a being" (BT, 9) ["*Sein ist jeweils das Sein eines Seienden*" (SZ, 9)]. Although there is a difference between being and beings, the terms cannot be thought without the other. As Heidegger notes, "we think of Being rigorously only when we think of it in its difference with beings, and of beings in their difference with Being"

(*Identity and Difference*, 62). This chiastic relation, which is even more pronounced in the original German—"*Klar ist nur, daß es sich beim Sein des Seienden und beim Seienden des Seins jedesmal um eine Differenz handelt*" (*Identität und Differenz*, 33)—introduces a logic of "the indifference of identity and difference," or of "the identity of the different." In fact, what Heidegger calls the "modal indifference" between "eigenhood [*Eigentlichkeit*] or uneigenhood [*Uneigentlichkeit*]" in *Being and Time* (BT, 215/SZ, 232, revised translation) might well be taken to describe the logic of quantum theory: philosophical complementarity.

Quantisation is a mode of analyzing the operations of an "indifferent reality" by way of "its" collapse into a differentiating measurement. As for Heidegger, in the quantum logic "what is ontically nearest and familiar is ontologically [and epistemologically] the farthest, unrecognized [*das ontisch Nächste und Bekannte ist das ontologisch Fernste, Unerkannte*]" (BT, 4/SZ, 43. See also BT, 20/SZ, 225). The importance of the "formalism" of the ψ-function is that it mediates between these two extremes by way of the quantisation and thus complication of the notion of measurement as a mode of doing science *and* as a mode of living. The scientific formalization of the unmeasured "given" by way of the ψ-function, which describes that "given" mathematically as being in a state of superposition, might be said to address Being as the ontic side of the onto-ontological divide between Being and Beings. It formalizes and thus models "given reality."

In order to "make sense," however, the ψ-function must be collapsed. In that state, the ψ-function addresses "the given as given" or, in Heidegger's terms, as the Being of a being [*das Sein* as *Seiendes*]. Together, the two complementary aspects make up an ontology and an epistemology that is both adequate to reality and at the same time qualifies as what Heinz von Foerster calls an "eigentheory." The "given is given" to the observer in a state of infinite differentiation, which means, as an infinity of actualized—as in: measured—eigenstates. As the observer to whom the "given is given" is immanent to the given, however, there is no clear break between observer and reality. In fact, to invoke such a break would lead back to a naïve, if now tragically naïve, realism. There is, however, an internal cut within the general complementarity of the onto-epistemological realm. In 1927, both quantum theory and philosophy are concerned with the relation between the given and the "given as given" in terms of "Quantisation as a Problem of Proper Values:" ψ-philosophy.

In the Schrödinger equation, a particle is described from within the parameters of a wave function. In this context, Bohr's description of complementarity in the context of two modes of waves is instructive. Like most of today's interpretations, and as implied by Schrödinger, Bohr considers the quantum state, i.e. the wave, to be the more inclusive image of physical reality. Under appropriate conditions, waves can show features of particle-like behavior. It is not so much that particles sometimes behave like waves, which was what brought about the initial wonder, but rather that waves sometimes behave like particles. A communal, quantitative superposition diffracts into individual, qualified eigenvalues.

In this context, consider Bohr's evocation of the notion of contraction to describe how, "at infinity" particle and wave are identical. On one end of the spectrum, Bohr posits "an *infinitely* narrow wave packet with a perfectly well-defined position" (Barad, *Meeting the Universe Halfway*, 298, emphasis added), which is "[c]lassically [. . .] how we think of a particle" (298). On the other end of the spectrum, he posits "an elementary monochromatic" wave, which is "spread out evenly across all of space" (298), as in: smeared across reality.

In terms of eigenvalues, the first, infinitely dense wave has, "almost" like a particle, a discrete eigenvalue, while the second wave, which consists of one frequency component only, does not. It is a "white wave," or, from a complementary point-of-view, a "pink wave." In terms of nineteenth-century topology, which was well-known to Bohr, one might say that Bohr stretches the complementarity of particle and wave out on a conceptual "projective plane" on which, at infinity, the formal opposites—an infinitely narrow wave and an infinitely wide, monochromatic wave—are "identified." The opposites are reconciled on an inherently paradoxical, complementary surface of thought.

A world made up of a tangle of assembled "particles and waves" consists of an infinity of fractal eigenvalues. In such a world, both the state of pure particle and pure wave are abstract idealizations. Human and non-human entities show both individual behavior and communal interference phenomena. Particles are in superposition, coherences are open to and in resonance with their milieu and the overall medium. In the following, I will formally, when it is not quoted, refer to the milieu as "the medium thought of as having eigenvalues" and to the medium as "the milieu thought of as having no eigenvalues." In relation to an entity, "its" medium is what Félix Guattari calls a "Cutout" (*Schizoanalytic Cartographies*, 56–57) from the overall "media multiplicity."

To sum up. All three modes of quantum theory imply the disruption of a naïve realism that maintains that a given eigenvalue can be measured numerically with "absolute determinacy" (Schrödinger, "Present Situation,"

152) and "*complete exactness*" (153). For all versions of quantum mechanics, it is only after their measurement that systems can be said to have an individual, discrete eigenstate and eigenvalue. In fact, before the measurement one cannot even speak of discrete particles or systems with specific eigenvalues. In other words, the process of measuring literally constructs singular eigenvalues from an overall superposition of eigenstates and thus it constructs discrete systems. What is conceptualized as a continuous, communal, and "virtual" eigenstate is actualized into a discontinuous, discrete, and "actual" eigenstate. The measurement turns the smeared cat into a cat that is either dead or alive. Although it collapses the virtual potentiality of a communal eigenstate into an actual, individual eigenstate, it trails that communal state behind and remains itself immanent to it.

If one considers every perceptual apparatus to be a complex measuring device, it is not that "given" systems are measured, but rather, as Schrödinger maintained, that systems are constructed through "their" measurement. When I talk, in what follows, of "systems," "entities," "objects," or "consistencies," it should thus be kept in mind that this is, in many senses, a misnomer.

Let me end this passage with an extremely evocative and quite beautiful quote by Heisenberg. "In the experiments about atomic events we have to do with things and facts, with phenomena that are just as real as any phenomena in daily life. But the atoms or the elementary particles themselves are not as real; they form a world of potentialities or possibilities rather than one of things or facts" (160). In terms of media studies, might media be considered as fields of potentiality from which forms and facts are assembled? As fields of affordances? Perhaps one might start thinking of media and forms not only as formally different but as complementary. Maybe it is time for "the quantisation of media studies as an eigenvalue problem."

For Schrödinger, the electron's discrete frequencies in the atomic spectra are not due to discontinuous transitions—to quantum jumps— but to resonance phenomena. As Bohr notes, "Schrödinger, in a recent paper (*Ann. d. Phys.*, 83, p. 956; 1927), emphasises the fact that the discontinuous exchange of energy between atoms required by the quantum postulate, from the point of view of the wave theory, is replaced by a simple resonance phenomenon" ("Quantum Postulate," 586). Bohr specifically mentions Schrödinger's "hope of constructing a pure wave theory without referring to the quantum postulate" (589); a future theory that is taken up by Barad's vision of "fields without collapse."

In the light of this comment, let me shift to resonance phenomena, which are easier to telescope into a macroscopic state than the quantum logic and a further field within physics where the concept of eigenvalues is important, in particular in reference to the notion of "eigenfrequency." Within resonant systems, an eigenfrequency is the frequency with which a system swings after an initial excitation, so that under ideal conditions, the eigenfrequency, also called "natural frequency," and the resonating frequency are identical. A practical use of such "eigenfrequencies" concerns the testing of materials. As each object resonates with a specific and invariant internal eigenfrequency when it is brought to vibrate, in mass-produced objects, differences in frequency point directly to material irregularities within the series. As in the case of a glass, a hollow metal object that is not flawed will ring when it is struck. In both cases, a dull sound points to a flaw that has caused the object's eigenfrequency to change. The question of seriality, therefore, pertains to how to model objects in terms of eigenfrequencies.

If identical objects have—at least from a macroscopic perspective— the "same" eigenfrequency, any object in a series that has a different eigenfrequency is presumably faulty, or, expressed less judgmentally, peculiar. It is "eigen." Such testing is particularly important for objects such as tuning forks, which need to have identical eigenfrequencies, such as the concert pitch of 440 hertz.

In general, musical harmonies, such as those that apply to overtones, are intimately related to eigenfrequencies and their scalar multiples. Already in 1863 Hermann von Helmholtz used the term *Eigentöne*— usually translated as "proper tones"—to define "tones of strongest resonance" (*Sensations of Tone*, 90). Once more, Alexander J. Ellis' translation of eigentones as "proper tones" veils the term's origins in the logic of eigenvalues and thus makes it difficult to "hear" many of its conceptual resonances.

Although they are pockets of temporal and spatial invariance and stability within a more comprehensive field of frequencies, eigenfrequencies resonate with the overall media multiplicity. In fact, all resonance phenomena rely on media in that "*resonance conveys energy*" (Cramer, *Symphonie*, 54): "A wave needs a medium in order to propagate itself, for a liquid wave it is the water, for the sound it is generally the air, for light the electromagnetic field (which used to be called aether), for earthquakes the crust of the earth" (53). Sound waves, for instance, "are transported by the medium of air, which is brought to resonate and conveys these vibrations to an object of appropriate frequency that is able to vibrate" (65). As Niels Bohr noted about the idealization inherent in

Schrödinger's idea of a general theory of resonance, "[t]he use of simply harmonic proper vibrations [*Eigenschwingungen*] in the interpretation of observations means, therefore, only a suitable idealisation which in a more rigorous discussion must always be replaced by a group of harmonic vibrations, distributed over a finite frequency interval" ("Quantum Postulate," 588). In physical reality, eigenfrequencies and eigenvibrations are always in resonance with other eigenvibrations with which they are in a state of superposition.

As a rule, far-from-equilibrium systems are more sensitive to minute perturbations within the material medium of that landscape of frequencies than equilibrious ones. The Tacoma Bridge disaster is a famous example of frequency interference between a system's eigenfrequency and the more comprehensive landscape of frequencies around it. It concerns what is called, in terms of physics, a resonance catastrophe, which designates "in mechanics and construction the destruction of a building or a technical installation through vibration. The cause for this is resonance: The energy is optimally conveyed by periodic excitation and it is stored in the system. Through this storage and the further input of energy, the system's vibrations increase until the breaking point is reached" (Cramer, 53). If "resonance consists in that vibrations enter into correlation and interfere with each other" (53) and if, when "waves of equal frequency run into each other, their antinodes strengthen" (53), it sometimes happens that "vibrations within the system synchronize to such a degree, get so much into step, that their amplitudes reinforce each other and become so strong that they bring the whole system to burst asunder" (80). Invariably, such resonance catastrophes happen "unexpectedly, suddenly, unpredictably" (84).

In *Differential Equations and Their Applications*, Michel Braun provides the following account and explanation of the disaster: "The Tacoma Bridge was built in 1940. From the beginning, the bridge would form small waves like the surface of a body of water. [...] At one point, one edge of the road was 28 feet higher than the other edge. Finally, this bridge crashed into the water below. One explanation for the crash is that the oscillations of the bridge were caused by the frequency of the wind being too close to the natural frequency of the bridge. The natural frequency of the bridge is the eigenvalue of smallest magnitude of a system that models the bridge. This is why eigenvalues are very important to engineers when they analyze structures" (171–173).

The cause of the catastrophe is reminiscent of an experiment by Helmholtz, who mounted two identical tuning forks on unconnected resonance cases. When he brought one of them to sound, the other sounded as well in what he called "sympathetic response" or "sympathetic resonance." Similarly, at a specific moment, the frequency of the vibrations that were triggered by the wind was in tune—"of an equal frequency" or "on the same wavelength"—with the eigenfrequency of the bridge, which picked up and responded to this frequency, like a radio or a television picks up waves that are transmitted on a specific frequency. This brought about a change in the general landscape of frequencies. When the eigenfrequency of the bridge began to resonate with the identical eigenfrequency of the wind, the resulting amplification in the overall landscape of frequencies brought the system of the bridge to a crucial point at which the internal stresses became so strong that the bridge's material and structural "threshold of tolerance" (Bateson, *Mind and Nature*, 59) was crossed. This resulted in the loss of its structural stability and of its definition as an invariant system. In systemic terms, it lost its alignment with the overall landscape of frequencies within which it was suspended. As Humberto Maturana and Francisco Varela will call it, it lost its structural coupling to the milieu. Similar catastrophes have been brought about by large groups of people marching across a bridge—a fact that might be read as a commentary on the physics of fascism—or when the "heart rate variability," which denotes minor, aperiodic variations in the rhythm of the heart, cease and the heart begins to beat in a completely periodic manner. In fact, whenever living systems become fully periodic, something tends to be seriously wrong.

Few resonance catastrophes are as spectacular as that of the Tacoma Bridge. In fact, at any given moment the world's overall landscape of frequencies is defined by an infinity of resonance catastrophes that happen on an infinity of levels. From a human scale, most of these are not perceived as catastrophic. In fact, most are not perceived by humans at all. Also, as long as it remains in an overall metastable equilibrium, the world is defined by "harmonious" frequency interferences. What all of this means is that *a system is not only in reference with its milieu, but also, and more immediately, in resonance with it.*

Earlier, I had noted that in terms of media studies the state of superposition in the logic of the complementarity of particle and wave might be taken to also define a state in which form and medium are dissolved into each other and thus quite literally indifferent. It was only by differentiating, at the moment of the collapse of the ψ-function, that a specific eigenvalue was created that functioned as a marker of form. From a position of a general theory of resonances, another way of conceptualizing the difference between medium and form is in terms of the resonances between a given multiplicity of unordered frequencies and an ordered multiplicity of eigenfrequencies. In both cases, the question is about the implications of these logics for media studies. Can Schrödinger's model help media studies in terms of their distinction between medium and form? And further, can one conceive of a media studies set in the conceptual landscape of resonances that Schrödinger envisioned in terms of the behavior of atoms?

Chapter 3

CYBERNETICS: 1946

In 1929, the mathematician and physicist John von Neumann, who had worked with David Hilbert in Göttingen from 1926 to 1927 and who would become a seminal figure in cybernetics, publishes a paper on the "General Eigenvalue Theory Hermitescher Functional Operators" [*"Allgemeine Eigenwerttheorie Hermitescher Funktionaloperatoren"*] in which he defines the term eigenfunction as "a number for which there is a function $f \neq 0$ with $Rf = \lambda f$; f is then eigenfunction" (50). In the same paper, von Neumann also talks of a series of eigenvalues as an "eigenseries [*Eigenfolge*]" (52).

In his 1948 dissertation *Das Gedächtnis: Eine quantenphysikalische Untersuchung*, Heinz von Foerster, another prominent figure in second-order cybernetics, proposes a mathematization of the function of memory on the background of Schrödinger's ψ-function: "In analogy to the notion to understand the 'GEN', the carrier of genetic characteristics [*Erbmerkmale*], as a quantum state of a large molecule (aperiodic crystal), which was developed by Delbrück, Schrödinger and others, the 'MEM', carrier of memory characteristics [*Erinnerungsmerkmale*], is understood as a microcomplex that can take on different quantum states" (1). What these two examples show is the strong presence of quantum physics and the concomitant references to eigenvalues in cybernetics.

In mathematics and physics, a system's eigenvectors, eigenvalues, and eigenfrequencies denote its invariants while it undergoes changes within a larger, itself continually shifting field. From the non-systemic side, they are what is subtracted from the overall, infinite multiplicity and dynamics of that given field. Although the two fields are often superposed, mathematics considers eigenvalues mainly in terms of abstract and immaterial functions while physics considers them in terms of concrete and material objects. In both cases, however, the eigenvalues in question concern inanimate systems.

When second-order cybernetics takes up the term eigenvalue, it extends its range of application to the animate world, in which living beings show both physical and psychic eigenbehavior [*Eigenverhalten* or *Eigenschaften*]. In Gregory Bateson's terms, second-order cybernetics crosses the "dividing line between the world of the living (where *distinctions* are drawn and *differences* can be a cause) and the world of nonliving billiard balls [...]. The difference between the physical world of pleroma, and the *creatura*" (*Mind and Nature*, 7).

The cybernetic interest in the cognitive aspects of living entities brings a decidedly systemic perspective to the discussion and it intensifies the debate about observation and the observer. It also adds a number of new eigenalloys to the discussion that are especially prominent in the work of German sociologist Niklas Luhmann, whose systems theory is in many ways inspired by second-order cybernetics and who specifically references the influence of Hilbert on von Foerster (*Gesellschaft 1*, 388, fn 42; *Gesellschaft 2*, 403, fn 43; see also Bryant, *Democracy of Objects*, 139). As Luhmann notes, living beings can be described by parameters such as "independent mobility [*Eigenbeweglichkeit*]" (*Gesellschaft 1*, 114), "endogenous dynamics [*Eigendynamik*]" (*Gesellschaft 2*, 80), "self-interest [*Eigeninteresse*]" (*Gesellschaft 2*, 248), and "own perception [*Eigenwahrnehmung*]" (*Gesellschaft 1*, 114) as the being's "internal performance [*Eigenleistung*]" (*Gesellschaft 2*, 330).

All of these eigenalloys define entities that come into existence by making distinctions, such as the one between inside and outside. In fact, their "independence [*Eigenständigkeit*]" (*Gesellschaft 1*, 272) results from making both conscious and unconscious differentiations. As "that which differentiates," the entity, somewhat like Schrödinger's observer, creates its environment [*Umwelt*] considered as the "collapsed milieu."

In cybernetics, the term "eigenorganization" (von Foerster, "Cybernetics," 311) denotes a specific *process*. To align "process and structure," or, more philosophically, "becoming" and "being," I will also use the term to denote the *entities* that result from that process. These entities show eigenbehavior, which denotes an eigenorganization's specific structural and behavioral characteristics [*Eigenarten* or *Eigenschaften*]. What links the terms eigenorganization and eigenbehavior is that both shift the explanation of systemic operations from essences to habits and from structure to process.

The conceptual ground of second-order cybernetics is the notion of cognition as a form of computation. Its world consists of what von Foerster calls "trivial" and "non-trivial" machines. While trivial machines are characterized by a built-in invariance or periodicity, which means that they show "an unambiguous relation between its input (stimulus, cause, etc.) and its output (reaction, effect, etc.)" (*Wissen*, 357), non-trivial machines are inherently ambiguous and defined by a built-in variance or a-periodicity. Two "identical" inputs may lead to significantly different outputs. "A reaction to a given stimulus that has been observed once does not have to happen again when, at a later point in time, the same stimulus occurs again" (247). Whereas trivial machines are predictable, non-trivial ones are unpredictable "ambiguity machines."

While inanimate machines can be non-trivial, animate machines are by definition non-trivial. In a biological context, the functioning of non-trivial machines is defined by a "computational interval" between stimulus and response. Varela will go as far as to maintain that, because it transforms stimuli into sets of data, any such interval can be considered as a rudimentary brain. In terms of media studies, these intervals separate medium from form. The cognitive faultline, thus, runs between forms that deal in discrete and differentiated data and media that deal in undifferentiated intensities. Instead of concerning the two extremes of data-to-data transfer and intensity-to-intensity transfer, the media faultline concerns transfers from intensity to data and from data to intensity.

The distance and difference between these might be said to increase with the complexity of the system and the concomitant unpredictability of the observer's internal operations. As von Foerster notes, "[t]he ur-sensomotoric cells of ur-sponges, hydras, or very early multicellular organisms are directly coupled with a contractive element. If you tickle a hydra with an acid, it immediately draws itself in—like a trivial machine" (*Beginning*, 97). If these systems became more complex, "the motor and the sensory elements became distanced from each other, they grew apart from each other in space. [. . .] over time the distance became too great, so an intermediate element stepped in. In physiology, this is called internuntius or internuntii, intermediate messenger and messengers, respectively. And this intermediary suddenly transformed this trivial system [. . .] into a completely and totally nontrivial system" (98). Although modern biology maintains that entities that might initially be considered as simple are in actual fact extremely complex, one may still maintain that less complex organisms are "almost directly" coupled to incoming stimuli from the medium while more complex forms are coupled more indirectly. Their interactions with the medium, one might say, are "more mediated."

A more-of-mediation implies the emergence of the agency of memory and it introduces "eigentimes:" individual senses of time and duration. A trivial machine needs neither a cognitive nor a systemic memory, because it will invariably react identically to a given stimulus.

It has no perception of duration. A non-trivial machine, however, needs both a cognitive and a systemic memory in order to adapt its present to its future behavior, an argument that is supported from a mathematical standpoint by Schrödinger ("Free Will," 14). In computational terms, the relation between input and output in a non-trivial machine "is not invariant, but determined by the earlier operations of the machine" (von Foerster, *Wissen*, 358). As "a once-observed reaction to a given stimulus does not have to reoccur at a later point in the presence of the same stimulus" (247), non-trivial machines are "variation machines" that are set against trivial stimulus–response machines.

In a number of ways, the coming-into-being of eigenorganizations recapitulates that of eigenvalues and eigenvectors. It is defined by processes of coherencing, consistencing, or crystallization, which is a terminology von Foerster took up from Schrödinger when he talked in his dissertation of "aperiodic crystals" in reference to the "quantum state of a large molecule." As I noted earlier, the first step toward such a coming-into-being is the development of a common vectorial orientation of heterogeneous elements; in mathematic terms of the creation of eigenvectors and eigenvalues. Through the development of both physical and psychic routines, habits or conventions, consistencies gradually close themselves off, both cognitively and physically, from their milieu. In terms of eigenvalues: through recursive operations— operations that operate back onto themselves—a field contracts around a number of invariant eigenvectors and eigenvalues. As von Foerster notes, "[i]f a nontrivial system operates in a closed unit, it gets to emergence, eigenbehaviors occur" (*Beginning*, 49). The gradual genesis of an eigenorganization, then, lies in habit formation by way of repeated operations and routines. Cybernetically speaking, eigenvalues come into being when certain functional and formal operations reproduce the "identical" value upon every re-entry into the functional formalism. "[U]nder certain conditions there exist indeed solutions which, when reentered into the formalism, produce again the same solution. These are called 'eigen-values,' 'eigen-functions,' 'eigen-behaviors,' etc., depending on which domain this formation is applied—the domain of numbers, in functions, in behaviors" (Segal, 145; see also von Foerster, *Wissen*, 260).

Against this conceptual background, eigenorganizations might be described as non-trivial consistencies that have, by way of recursive operations, contracted around an invariant eigenvalue. By way of feedback-loops with the medium in which they operate, they have settled, both temporally and spatially, into a state of systemic equilibrium.

"If I want to achieve 'thoughts at peace,' then I'll run through recursive operators toward a stability" (*Beginning*, 178), von Foerster muses. Within their specific eigenspaces, eigenorganizations are quite literally the embodiment—the material memory, so to speak—of the set of recursive operations, which, within an overall functional envelope, create "functional [...] operational [...], structural states of stability" (*Wissen*, 107) that are tied to invariance. "Pragmatically, these states correspond to the computation of the invariants, be these object-constancy, perceptual universals, cognitive invariants, identifications, names etc. Of course one must also mention here the classical cases of ultrastability and homeostasis" (75): *et in arcadia ego*.

A basic conceptual tenet of second-order cybernetics concerns what it calls the "informational and operational closure" of eigenorganizations. On the cognitive side, this implies that information is not something that is given "out there" and that comes to the system from that outside. As Schrödinger had noted, there are no values before the measurement. In fact, the prerequisites for the creation and emergence of information is that an entity has developed eigenvalues and an operational stability: "I am capable—through the attempt at closure of an operative unit or the peeling-out of an operative unit through closure—of reaching stable eigenvalues, eigenbehaviors, so that I allow information to emerge for me out of this situation. The information was not in the game to begin with, the results were only won once stabilities were able to develop" (*Beginning*, 28). More laconically, "the moment I introduce the idea of a distinction, there must also be a mechanism that can make a distinction" (71). When Luhmann talks, somewhat ironically and paradoxically, of "contingency as the eigenvalue of modern society" (*Kontingenz*, 93), he can do so because, as von Foerster notes, "eigenvalues create, because of their self-defining (or self-creating) nature, topological 'closure'" (*Wissen*, 108).

The genesis of eigenorganizations can thus be conceptualized as the gradual, both material and immaterial contraction and consolidation of a field of density; as the emergence of vortices from turbulence by way of habitual movements around centers of attraction. For von Foerster, "strange attractors" (*Wissen*, 261, 296) are in fact nothing but a new and, in his view, a less elegant conceptualization *of* and terminology *for* eigenvalues. As Manuel DeLanda notes in *A Thousand Years of Nonlinear History*, eigenorganizations are "dynamical systems that endogeneously generate their own *stable states* (called 'attractors' or 'eigenstates')" (63).

Jean-Pierre Dupuy had already taken up this analogy in "Philosophy and Cognition: Historical Roots," where he notes that "[a] given network usually possesses a multiplicity of self-behaviors, or as they are sometimes called 'attractors' (a term borrowed from dynamical systems theory), and converges toward one or another depending on the initial conditions of the network. The 'life' of a network can thus be conceived as a trajectory through a 'landscape' of attractors, passing from one to another as a result of perturbations or shocks from the external world" (553).

Ultimately, second-order cybernetics is less interested in the mathematics of a living being's "computational capacities" than "in its 'self-behaviors' (or *eigenbehaviors*, to use the hybrid English-German phrase of quantum mechanics, from which systems theory borrowed the concept) [...] Like every automaton with an internal state, a network calculates its state in the next period as a function of its state during the current period. [...] Note that these external events come to acquire meaning in the context of the network as a result of the network's own activity: the *content*—the meaning—which the network attributes to them is precisely the self-behavior, or attractor, that results from them. Obviously, then, this content is purely endogenous, and not the reflection of some external 'transcendent' objectivity" (553).

If I noted that recursive operations indicate the creation and gradual stabilization of a consistency, that consistency is "in actual fact" nothing but the set of invariant values that result from these recursive operations. In this context, "invariant" does not refer to a given identity but to the fact that the values keep the coherency within a specific computational envelope and thus allow for the stability needed to maintain what Gregory Bateson calls "*pattern[s] through time*" (*Mind and Nature*, 14).

At this point of my discussion, let me propose another superposition of science and philosophy. What if one were to consider recursive computational iterations as "computational habits"? As inherently habitual, eigenvalues mark consistencies within multiplicitous phase spaces that are defined by parameters that range from the mathematical to the cultural. In *Parables for the Virtual*, Brian Massumi in fact describes almost literally von Foerster's notion of habitual computation. "Habit is an acquired automatic self-regulation. It resides in the flesh. Some say in matter. As acquired, it can be said to be 'cultural.' As automatic and material, it can pass for 'natural'" (11).

While such a superposition helps to conceptualize eigenorganizations without recourse to notions of essence or substance, one should be aware that habits can easily harden into stable, quasi-essentialist routines. If certain habits become addictive—if a habit becomes too much of a habit, that is—the system loses its plasticity. As Bateson notes, "in the ongoing life of the organism there is a process of sorting, which in some of its forms is called 'habit formation.' In this process, certain items, which have been learned at 'soft' levels, gradually become 'hard'" (*Sacred Unity*, 138).

As William James notes, while habits allow for movement and change, they are simultaneously "the enormous fly-wheel of society, its most precious conservative agent. It alone is what keeps us all within the bounds of ordinance" (*Principles*, 121). The good thing about habits is that they are softer and more plastic than "immutable laws," the bad thing is that often they are too hard for the entity to be able to easily kick them.

I have put "immutable laws" into quotation marks because according to a habitual logic, there are no immutable, essential laws. Even natural laws are nothing but habits of nature that describe systems with quasi-stable eigenvalues. As Charles Sanders Peirce maintains, "habit is by no means exclusively a mental fact. Empirically, we find that some plants take habits. The stream of water that wears a bed for itself is forming a habit" ("Survey," 342). Similarly, William James notes that "[n]ature exhibits only changes, which habitually coincide with one another so that their habits are discernible in simple 'laws'" (*Radical Empiricism*, 74). As Brian Massumi expresses it, "[b]oth Hume, the inventor of empiricism, and C.S. Peirce, the inventor of the pragmatism further developed by James, argued that nature does not follow laws. *Laws follow nature*. What nature does is generate surprises and contract habits" (247).

The reason why one can superpose a physical theory of habits and a philosophical theory of psychic habit formation is that both the creation of sets of physical and psychic habits can quite literally be described as the creation of eigenvalues. Already James noted that because "the law of habit [...] is a material law" (*Principles*, 126), "the philosophy of habit is [...], in the first instance, a chapter in physics rather than in physiology or psychology" (105).

Like differentiation, habit formation considered as the creation of eigenvalues and eigenvectors is inherent to all living matter. "Can't," Massumi asks, "the self-organizations of matter described by chaos theory also be considered habits? Aren't they inhumanly contracted habits of matter? [...] Is there a difference in kind or only a difference in mode or degree between the inhuman habits of matter and the human ones?" (237). Or, as Peirce proposed, "[m]ay not the laws of physics be habits gradually acquired by systems?" ("Design," 553).

Peirce's proposition in turn resonates with James' belief that "[t]he laws of Nature are nothing but the immutable habits which the different elementary sorts of matter follow in their actions and reactions upon each other. In the organic world, however, the habits are more variable than this" (*Principles*, 104). Laws, therefore, are invented or abstracted from fields of habitual change.

Gilles Deleuze also proposes that "the subject is constituted within the given" (*Empiricism*, 104) by way of habit formation. In terms of the natural elements, if "[i]n essence, habit is contraction" (Deleuze, *Difference*, 73), every organism may be said to be contracted from specific physical and biochemical habits; from an inherently "intelligent matter" that is defined by perceptual and cognitive operations. This is why Deleuze can state that "[w]e are made of contracted water, earth, light and air" (*Difference*, 73) and could argue that this process of contraction intertwines "all the habits of which it is composed" (75). The "lived reality of a sub-representative domain" (69) lies beneath the realm of observed reality like the lived reality of Schrödinger's cat lies beneath its observed reality.

Even during the passive, unconscious processes of contraction that constitute our "habit of living" (*Difference*, 74), an emergent consistency feeds back with these forces of physical contraction through processes of sub-individual psychic contemplation. These feedbacks are responsible for the constitution of a "passive self" that is nothing but the body of resonance of specific habits. It "contemplates and contracts the individuating factors of such fields [the 'pre-existing fields of individuation'] and constitutes itself at the points of resonance of their series" (276). It is "simultaneously through contraction that we are habits," therefore, and "through contemplation that we contract" (74). Even operations that seem to be "natural" are, in actual fact, what Peirce calls "inattentive habit[s]" ("Survey," 328) that operate on the same unconscious level as "perceptual judgements" ("Pragmatism and Abduction," 181).

According to this rigorously habitual logic, the psychic realm extends deeply into sub-individual levels and shades into unconscious physical and biochemical contractions and modifications. Into "our thousands of component habits" (Deleuze, *Difference*, 75). "[B]elow the level of active [conscious] syntheses" lies "the domain of passive syntheses which constitutes us, the domain of modifications, tropisms and little peculiarities" (79). As with Heisenberg's notion of an atomic world of "potentialities or possibilities," "[b]eneath the general operation of laws, [...] there always remains the play of singularities" (25).

As the subject is "a *habitus*, a habit, nothing but the habit in a field of immanence, the habit of saying I" (Deleuze, *Philosophy*, 48), it is in a "state of consistence" that originates temporally *in* and in logical terms is complementary *to*, planes of multiplicity such as the sonorous medium in terms of sound or the photonic medium in terms of light. The world as both lived and collapsed. The collapsed world within the lived world. As Deleuze notes, "[w]e start with atomic parts, but these atomic parts have transitions, passages, 'tendencies,' which circulate from one to another. These tendencies give rise to *habits*. Isn't this the answer to the question 'what are we?' We are habits, nothing but habits— the habit of saying 'I.' Perhaps there is no more striking answer to the problem of the Self'" (x).

To consider habit formation to be the basis of the construction of consistencies promises, from within a set of given systemic constraints of course, the possibility of unconditional change. If human beings are nothing but "walking bundles of habits" (James, *Principles*, 127), this ensures an evolutionary freedom that allows the entity to escape, at every instant, its current habitual envelope and defines eigenorganizations as the invariants in an ongoing process of contraction and contemplation around specific attractors. They come to consider the bundles of eigenvalues, eigenvectors, and eigenfrequencies, but also of eigentimes and eigenspaces, as their "self." Through iterated, habitual biochemical, informational, and mental operations, they have separated "themselves" from the infinitely complex multiplicity of the processual space that surrounds them. Or rather: they have not separated themselves, they are themselves the result of that separation.

As the relation between eigenorganizations and the milieu is analogous to that between forms and media, through these concentric, iterated, habitual operations, eigenorganizations take on, for other eigenorganizations, the character of stable objects or images with specific, inherent properties. As Luhmann notes, "objects appear as repeated indications, which, rather than having a *specific* opposite, are demarcated against 'everything else'" (*Art as Social System*, 46). When an eigenorganization registers recurrent operations in its milieu, it isolates these "habitual" operations from the larger set of stimuli that are constantly provided by that milieu, calling the result of these cutouts "objects." In von Foerster's terminology, "what is considered in an epistemology without observer [. . .] as an 'object' [*Gegen-Stand*] appears [*erscheint*] in an epistemology that includes an observer as [. . .] a sign of stable 'eigenbehavior'" (*Wissen*, 103).

Cognition, then, has to do not only with pattern recognition but also, and more importantly so, with pattern construction. In the same way that there is no information "in the wild," the "objects" that eigenorganizations register in their milieu are not first of all given objects or given patterns, but the result of their own internal perceptual and informational procedures and operations in response to recurring irritations. As Maturana notes, "we cannot *transfer* anything, but only send out sounds and hope that they find, in others, the desired resonance" (*Was ist Erkennen*, 204).

From sets of invariant irritations—what they call "patterns"—that impinge on them from the outside, eigenorganizations extrapolate and extract, through their specific eigenbehaviors and thus "autonomously [*eigenständig*]" (205)—by way of their specific modes of differentiation, that is—the habits or characteristics that come to define these recurrent stimuli for them as objects or eigenorganizations with specific qualities such as color, hardness, elasticity, or movement. If one were to read this as "Schrödinger translated into a different terminology," the ψ-function would be "contained" in the notion of "indistinct irritation." Like science, individualized life consists of constant operations of the digitalization— the measuring, one might say—of an analog reality. Humans constantly "collapse" the stimulating world according to specifically human parameters.

Perceptually and cognitively, then, "objects," considered as particles with specific eigenstates, are constructed within the observing system. They are the mental markers or tokens of extremely complex bundles of recurrent irritations considered as "waves of energy." In other words, some of the perceived vectors remain stable even while they show dynamic behavior. As with eigenfaces, a specific bundle of irritations that is perceived as having a stable density, electromagnetic frequency, and extension, is marked as a table, a chair, or a face. Eigenvalues are thus not only relevant in that eigenorganizations are themselves *eigen*constructed, but also in that their psychic reality is, as a result of this eigenconstruction, an "eigenreality" and their cognitive world an "eigenworld."

Cognition, then, is the extrapolation and extraction of objects from the milieu by way of an entity's eigenbehavior. This extraction is reductive in that it entails the conversion of an infinite causal nexus into a finite one. As von Foerster notes, "[t]he crucial contribution of cybernetics to epistemology is the possibility of the metamorphosis of an open into a closed system, in particular the closure of the linear, open, *infinite* causal nexus into a closed and *finite* one" (*Wissen*, 51, emphasis added). Operationally, von Foerster argues, that reduction is necessary. "Eigen behavior generates discrete, identifiable entities. Producing discreteness out of infinite variety has incredibly important consequences. It permits us to begin naming things. Language is the possibility of carving out of an infinite number of possible experiences those experiences which allow stable interactions of yourself with yourself" (Segal, 128). As Schrödinger had noted, measurement is indeed unavoidable. "There is no ψ-function in life."

Eigenorganizations reduce the multiplicity of the surrounding milieu by both recognizing and realizing recurrent patterns in it and by isolating these patterns from what they perceive as an overall patternless movement. For an eigenorganization, therefore, objects are not only the result of these objects' actions and eigenbehavior. As they impinge upon the system merely as sets of more or less invariant irritations, they are also the result of the eigenorganization's own eigenbehavior and, as such, merely "*tokens* for eigen behaviors. [...] In the cognitive realm, objects are the token names we give to our eigen behavior. [...] This is the constructivist's insight into what takes place when we talk about our experience with objects" (Segal, 127–128). As Bateson states, "[e]xperience of the exterior is always mediated by particular sense organs and neural pathways. To that extent, objects are my creation, and my experience of them is subjective, not objective" (*Mind and Nature*, 31). Or, as Luhmann takes up von Foerster, "[t]he perceived world is thus nothing but the totality of the 'eigenvalues' of neurophysiological operations" (*Kunst der Gesellschaft*, 15).

Luhmann's systems theory, which takes its notion of the observer directly from second-order cybernetics, argues that "[e]igenvalues" (*Wissenschaft*, 113) and thus "stable eigenstates [*Eigenzustände*]" (321) are created through the recursive operation of "observations of observations," which means that the repetition of the operation of identification must succeed in "condensing [*kondensieren*]" (312) "that which is taken to be identical" (312). Through these condensations, "the system computes its 'eigenvalues' and identifies identity as a sign for such eigenvalues, and by way of eigenvalues it can organize eigenaction [*Eigenverhalten*]" (312). In this way, "[t]he system solidifies [*festigt*] 'eigenstates' and thus gains a dynamic stability" (320).

As science is a recursive operation that is ultimately tied to what happens in the field of structural couplings, and thus to what cannot be observed or described, it cannot develop an "eigenrationality" (670). All it can produce are "[r]elatively stable 'eigenstates'" (670). Once more, this is a deeply pragmatic procedure. "Instead of taking recourse to ultimate unities, one observes observations, one describes descriptions. On the second-order level, there are once more recursive relations and searches for 'eigenvalues,' which do no longer change during the further operations of the system" (717).

As these perceptual operations are recursive, eigenvalues develop over time. In fact, Luhmann suggests that we might follow George Herbert Mead and Alfred North Whitehead, who "assigned a function to identifiable and recognizable objects, whose primary purpose is to bind time. This function is needed because the reality of experience and actions consists in mere event sequences" (*Art as Social System*, 46–47).

In cognitive registers, then, objects are "nothing but the *eigenbehaviors* of observing systems that result from using and reusing their previous distinctions" ("Deconstruction," 768). Or, as von Foerster maintains, "[e]igenvalues have been found ontologically to be discrete, stable, separable and composable, while ontogenetically to arise as equilibria that determine themselves through circular processes. Ontologically, Eigenvalues and objects, and likewise, ontogenetically, stable behavior and the manifestation of a subject's 'grasp' of an object cannot be distinguished" (*Wissen*, 109).

The circular perceptual and cognitive processes Luhmann focuses on are not, however, enough to qualify eigenorganizations as living entities. Even while eigenorganizations are informationally and operationally closed off from their surroundings, they are simultaneously energetically open to, and thus entangled with, these surroundings. From this perspective, the surroundings are not understood as the world they construct and, in the case of humans, the one they project as a set of mental images [*Vorstellungen*], but as the one within which and out of which they are constructed and to which they remain immanent even while being informationally and operationally closed-off from it. They denote the world in which their living unfolds and is realized.

While eigenorganizations are closed off from the field of energy and intensity in terms of operation and information, they are, in energetic terms, dissipative, open, temporally negentropic entities that interact with a multiplicity of given intensities in the sense of "indifferent" forces. This openness implies that energetically, their overall biological history is subjected to an entropic decline. In the following, I will use the term "energy" to refer to actualized intensity and "energetic potentiality" to refer to a state of difference *of* and *in* intensity. "Intensity" refers to "the given," "energy" to "intensity in a state of the given as given." As such, energy is qualified intensity—intensity in a state of extensity.

The challenge posed by conceptualizing the simultaneity of informational and operational closure and energetic openness is to think from within a paradoxical logic according to which physical and metaphysical registers are simultaneously operative, although they concern conceptually and formally separated levels. As von Foerster notes, "the term self-organization is the perhaps most general term for the description of these fascinating processes that take place in organizationally *closed*, but energetically (thermodynamically) *open* systems" (*Wissen*, 296, emphasis added).

To recapitulate: eigenorganizations function as differentiators between an informationally and operationally closed and an energetically open space. The field of information, operation, and measurements on the one hand and the field of irritation, intensity, and superposition on the other. They emerge from within a given multiplicity through processes of contraction and contemplation, crystallizing into consistencies through the repeated creation of operational and informational distinctions and the recursive computation and re-insertion of these distinctions into "themselves." The result of these recursive operations are eigenspaces in which they function with the aim of maintaining an overall, operational eigenvalue that consists of integrated, "differentiated" eigenvalues and of remaining within the range of operations that allow them to remain operative.

Although eigenvalues define entities as the result of internal operations and invariants within transformations, these operations depend on energetic perturbations and thus on changes in the medium they inhabit. If these stimuli become too strong to be integrated, an entity will no longer be able to operate within the tolerances that define its range of acceptable structural change and lose its overall coherence. In other words, when its overall eigenvalue is challenged, an entity can either adapt or change the milieu. If it does neither of the two, it will lose its internal structural stability and stop being that specific entity. Ultimately, eigenorganizations might thus be described as "the things formerly known as living beings." They are temporally equilibrious, semi-stable, eigenorganizing systems that operate within a medium from which they have separated themselves through recursive biochemical and informational operations but to which they remain energetically immanent. Their specific contour and character is the sum of their overall ecology of eigenvalues. What second-order cybernetics argues, therefore, is that *the difference of subject and object should be replaced by the difference between eigenorganization and intensity.*

At this point, let me introduce a distinction that I have until now tacitly assumed. By default, media studies define media as man-made technological devices that assemble, store, or transfer information, such as the telephone, the typewriter, the camera, or the computer, as well as earlier informational media such as the canvas, the book, or the single sheet of paper.

The pulp from which paper is made can function as a conceptual bridge to the notion of media that I have used in my text until now. This notion, which has been used mainly in the natural sciences is "formational" rather than "informational." It concerns both natural and perceptual media as environments, such as water for fish, air for humans, or a nutrient solution in a petri dish for bacteria.

If informational media are complicated technical machines whose strictly coupled parts combine toward very specific uses, these environments are multitudes of small, loosely coupled elements from which larger, more complex, and more strictly coupled devices are assembled. These elements form the "molecular" building blocks of the material as well as the immaterial world, and much of science is about their specific modes of assemblage. One of the projects for a future media studies is to align these two definitions.

Early texts that have introduced the definition of formational media into media studies are Fritz Heider's "Ding und Medium" from 1923 and "Thing and Medium" from 1959. These divergent versions of "one" article implicitly open up the question whether, if eigenvalues are markers of "form"—here understood as "things" or "objects"—are there states that are completely without eigenvalues? In Luhmann's terminology, are there states that are not only loosely coupled, but not coupled at all?

The conceptual "scattering" of the term eigenvalue into Heider's texts concerns light and sound as both natural media and as media of perception [*Wahrnehmungsmedien*]. "We do not perceive light waves as things that touch our eyes and refer to something else. We seem to see the mediated object directly" ("Thing," 2), Heider notes. In order to explain this fact, Heider differentiates between solid and semi-solid objects in our perceptual surrounding and "the air-filled space through which we see and hear" (6). The optical medium, he maintains, consists of "a manifold of light rays [*Lichtwellenmannigfaltigkeit*]" (7, 17; "Ding," 323), a photonic multiplicity that consists of "a multitude of rays of different directions" ("Thing," 16). This multiplicity is "formed" when the rays are reflected by the surface of an object whose image they carry and make visible. In analogy, the acoustic medium consists of a "manifold" (6) of sound waves.

Heider concludes that "the special state of the medium is *to a high degree* irrelevant for the form of the process in it" (4, emphasis added). As a not-at-all coupled set of elements—"[w]ave frequencies and other determinations are coupled only to a small degree, if at all", Heider notes (16)—the medium invariably takes on the specific form [*Eigenform*] ("Ding," 323) of the objects in which it actualizes itself. In direct reference to the theory of eigenvalues, Heider notes that, unlike the things within it, the medium does not have a "free vibration [*Eigenschwingung*]" ("Thing," 4; "Ding," 324) and thus it does not form a coherent unity [*Einheit*] (325). Its only characteristic, in fact, is to be without characteristics. It is a pure multiplicity made up of parts that are "independent of each other" ("Thing," 7). Light rays, for instance, form an "atomistic manifold [*ein atomistisches Nebeneinander*]" (19 "Ding," 332–333)].

This difference between "eigenhood" and "uneigenhood" is the categorical difference between form and medium. Things are unities with eigenforms and eigenfrequencies ["[*A*]*n den Dingen ist das echte Eigengeschehen, die Eigenschwingung*" (329)], while the medium can only be formed by forces external to it, such as the surface of a thing in the case of light or the striking of a tuning fork in the case of sound, both of which "force" the medium to take on a specific form.

Although "a forced vibration has the same geometrical characteristics as a free vibration" ("Thing," 6) and "appears to be unitary" (6), forced vibrations are "composite events" (5) that form "spurious units" (7), while "free vibration is a unitary event" (5) that is associated with a true unity. As Heider notes, "things show free vibrations, media show forced vibrations" (17).

The structural difference between things and media such as light and sound, therefore, is that between "eigenhood [*Eigentlichkeit*]" and "uneigenhood [*Uneigentlichkeit*]". Light, as an inherently formless carrier, is a "medium without qualities." "[F]ree vibration occurs in things, forced vibration in media" ("Thing," 15). From this, Heider concludes that light operates best, both in terms of perception and of information, when it is completely under erasure. Although "in the medium we find wave events and also movements of the small units" (13), these events are "irrelevant for the things of our order of magnitude" (13). As Heider notes, "neither molecular events nor wave events have coordinated effects within the thing order" (14).

The perceptual apparatus reconstructs the unity of the original things—what Heider calls "core events"—from the perception of the spurious unity of its mediated version, whether directly "in life" or from its traces within technical media such as a film or a phonograph, which Heider calls "offshoots." "It is the task of the apparatus of perception to construct out of the manifold of impinging offshoots something that is coordinated to core events" ("Thing," 34). This "reconstruction of the core events on the basis of the offshoots is a process of the 'synthesis of images out of sensations'" (25).

Heider's notion of an optical multiplicity is an important step toward the definition of a state without eigenvalues. In the light of the theory of eigenvalues, however, one should become much more sensitive to the ways in which light is always already formed and thus partakes of the formed things that it carries. Perhaps media such as light do not dissolve as easily and successfully into objects as Heider assumes. Rather than positing a state of multiplicity on the one end and of formation on the other, one would perhaps need to think of a way to align these "complementary opposites."

Such a theory of optical complementarity is given in Wolfgang Schöne's book *Über das Licht in der Malerei* [*On Light in Painting*], which deals with the insistence of light as a medium in painting. Schöne traces historical shifts in the theory of artistic light by differentiating between "eigenlight [*Eigenlicht*]", "lighting-light [*Beleuchtungslicht*]", and "eigencolor [*Eigenfarbe*]". Eigenlight, which defines the "light metaphysics" of medieval painting (109), refers to the light that seems to emanate from within a painting and whose luminosity radiates toward the spectator, which is why Schöne also calls it "sending light." The notion of eigenlight becomes most visible in the "eigenshine [*Eigenglanz*]" (25) of the golden backgrounds of icons, which embody the luminosity of a God who is "in a literal sense, light" (64).

Between the fifteenth and eighteenth centuries, this metaphysical logic of eigenlight is replaced by the physics of a lighting-light that can seem to originate either from without or from within pictorial space. Because it lights this space, Schöne also calls this light "showing light" (119), which he differentiates once more into a natural, an artificial, or a sacral light, as well as, in addition, into a light that is none of these, and which Schöne therefore calls "indifferent" (112) in relation to the three other categories. Between the fifteenth and eighteenth centuries, this "indifferent" light defines the passage from an inherently sacral light to the natural and artificial light that, together, will define the nineteenth century.

If, from medieval times to the nineteenth century "color was understood as a function of light" (208), in modern art, "light becomes a function of color" (200). Although each specific "corporeal color [*Körperfarbe*]" (201) has its own value within a spectrum from darkness and brightness—an "eigenbright [*Eigenhell*]" and an "eigendark [*Eigendunkel*]" such as a bright yellow opposed to a dark brown—its material color [*stoffliche Buntheit*] is structurally set against an overall immaterial luminosity [*immaterielle Helle*] (203). A light blue chair might look darker than a dark blue chair if the immaterial luminosity around it is low.

According to Schöne, in twentieth-century painting, the importance of the "local color" of bodies increases above that of the surrounding "local light," because the framework is no longer a "given" naturalism that is based on a poetics of figuration, but rather an abstract universe that is defined by the eigenvalue of specific colors. In the passage from figuration to abstraction, eigencolor takes over from eigenlight. In general, however, all of the historical phases define interplays of color and light, the most general question being "in the history of Western painting, how do the eigenvalues and representational values of color relate to the artistic medium [*Mittel*] of light?" (205).

It is difficult to conceive, categorically, of the pure local color of an object, because that would imply the complete erasure of both showing light and ambient light. In terms of the presentation of paintings, some modern museums attempt to approach such an ideal state by creating an ideally neutral architectural background and an equally ideal neutral light in which to hang their paintings; a light Schöne calls "site-light [*Standortlicht*]" (109). This is different in palaces such as the Palazzo Pitti or the Uffizi; pre-museal milieus in which the paintings shift with the ambient day- and nightlight, without ever coming to rest in an unchanging milieu of a fully artificial and unchanging light. Despite these attempts, the ambient light invariably interacts with the specific local color of objects. Here as well, the insistence of the medium in the object cannot be excluded except by creating completely closed-off, artificial milieus. In an open, luminist world, however, local color and local light invariably form complex optical mixtures and assemblages.

While the notion of "local color" denotes specific colors of specific objects as unmodified by ambient light and luminosity—the pigmented color of an object without the interference of its position within an overall optical milieu—the notion of "local light" includes ambient light as a medium that suffuse both the action and the objects that are being described. Ambient light does not only suffuse the world, however. It is the medium within which actions, objects, situation, and the world itself emerge.

Chapter 4

BIOLOGY: 1973

What if one were to stress, as Wolfgang Schöne does, the embodied complementarity of "thing" and "medium" rather than their formal difference? Although at first sight the biological theory of autopoiesis, which was developed by Humberto Maturana and Francisco Varela during the 1960s and 1970s, seems to underscore Heider's formalism, it provides, from a biological perspective, a conceptualization of the relation between medial multiplicity and formal complexity that recapitulates the various embodiments of the eigenlogic that I have discussed so far.

How does the theory of autopoiesis negotiate the relation between the eigen and the uneigen? In scientific terms, between a deterministic chaos and a pure chaos, or, as Michel Serres calls it, between pure and ordered multiplicities. With the notion that "the cosmos is not a structure, it is a pure multiplicity of ordered multiplicities and pure multiplicities" (*Genesis*, 11).

Deleuze and Guattari negotiate this relation, which they consider to lie at the heart of philosophy, as that between the "pure multiplicity" of the "Plane of Immanence" and the "ordered multiplicity" of the "Plane of Consistency." The Plane of Immanence is "a *virtual*, containing all possible particles and drawing out all possible forms, which spring up only to disappear immediately, without consistency or reference, without consequence. Chaos is an infinite speed of birth and disappearance. Now philosophy wants to know how to retain infinite speeds while gaining consistency, by *giving the virtual a consistency specific to it*" (*What is Philosophy?*, 118). As Guattari notes, this Plane of Immanence remains "[l]ike an aerosol, [...] in a state of suspension at the heart of the 'chaosmic' Plane of Consistency" (*Schizoanalytic Cartographies*, 155). Like wave and particle, in fact, the two planes—the planes of the uneigen and of the eigen—are complementary. "Entirely separated and yet pairing up unceasingly" (155).

For Maturana, the moment of the genesis of the complexity of the milieu from the multiplicity of the medium is instantaneous. Reaching back to the terminology of quantum theory, he notes that "organisation exists or does not exist, appears and vanishes again into nothing. It is 'digital,' not 'analog': Between Yes and No there is, if you want, a 'quantum jump,' without transition, without a mediating 'hardly' or 'a little'" (*Was ist Erkennen?*, 78, emphasis added). Although this might be taken to mean that chaos is replaced by order, in the same way that Heider had argued that the multiplicity of light rays vanishes in the luminous complexity of the world, in *The Embodied Mind: Cognitive Science and Human Experience*, Varela notes that as embodied, "organism and medium mutually specify each other" (197). This "*codetermination*" (198, original emphasis)—the reciprocal presupposition of organism and medium and the fact that they are "mutually unfolded and enfolded structures" (199)—implies that every one of its changes is deeply dependent both on the organism's history and on the overall weather of intensities understood as the set of probabilities that pertain to the milieu: "Pattern formation and morphogenesis are highly constrained cellular choreographies that drastically delimit the scope of possibilities for change" (189). What allows for an organism's agency and survival is the ability to avail itself of the milieu's potential energies, such as the ability of birds to use currents of air or the ability of surfers to fold themselves into the kinetic energy contained in a wave. "At any one moment in the system's history it is the *degree of intensity* of these parameters (the degree of temperature, pressure, volume, speed, density, and so on) that defines the attractors available to the system and, hence, the type of forms it may give rise to," Manuel DeLanda notes (263).

The diffraction of the logic of eigenvalues into the biosciences calls for the introduction of the neologism "autopoietic system" into the discussion—a term whose genesis Maturana and Varela describe in *Autopoiesis and Cognition: The Realization of the Living*. Like "eigenorganization," the term combines "self" [*auto*] and "creation" [*poiesis*]. In opposition to "allopoietic" systems, which are created and regulated from the outside, autopoietic systems are self-organizing and self-referential entities. Living, non-trivial machines.

What does "living" mean in this context? Like Schrödinger, Maturana and Varela do not claim to have an answer to "the question of life" or to "the origin of life." Rather, they are concerned with conceptualizing the inherent qualities of consistencies that we consider to be alive. In particular, the theory of autopoiesis looks at what it means to be alive from the perspective of individual life as a cybernetic process of self-organization and self-regulation as well as feedback with the milieu. After a digital moment of genesis and a process of systemic consolidation, autopoietic systems settle, for a specific period of time, during which they cohere, into a systemic equilibrium. For the duration of their individual life spans, they develop a set of invariant eigenvalues. Much of Maturana and Varela's work is concerned with providing detailed diagrams of the extremely complex physical, biochemical, and cognitive operations involved in these autopoietic processes.

The theory of autopoiesis shares with second-order cybernetics and systems theory the tenet that living entities are defined by the "*operational closure* in their organization" and the fact that "their identity is specified by a network of dynamic processes whose effects do not leave that network" (*Tree of Knowledge*, 89). In "Eigenbehavior: Some Algebraic Foundations of Self-Referential System Processes," Varela uses the term eigenbehavior to describe this systemic autonomy—"self-determined behavior" (170)—as the creation of invariant eigenstates "by way of recursion:" "I propose the name *eigenbehavior* for an expression in the mathematical sense described below that is intended to represent the autonomy of some concrete system" (170). Going back to Hilbert's initial mathematical use of the term "eigenvalue," Varela notes that "[e]igenbehaviors can be characterized as the fixed points of certain transformations" (171). It is that which remains "invariant" (171) within a field of continuous change and thus marks, within that change, systematicity.

In fact, Varela points out that "[t]his compound is a generalization consistent with the standard use of "eigenvalue" and "eigenvector" in linear algebra to denote certain fixed points in linear maps" (170). From this mathematical description, he then draws a vector to the term's use in biology and cybernetics. "N. Jerne (1974) introduced the idea as a qualitative characterization for the moment-to-moment stable state of the cellular interactions that specifies the immune network in living organisms. [. . .] Von Foerster's (1977) paper is entitled "Objects: tokens of eingenbehavior," and discusses the closure of the sensory-motor interactions in a nervous system, giving rise to perceptual regularities as objects" (170–171).

While eigenbehaviors result from recursive operations inside of the system, the theory of autopoiesis relates the closure to the system's structural couplings, which concern its openness to the medium and are "characterized by *fluxes* through its boundaries" (204). In fact, Varela sees the two perspectives as "*complementary* descriptions of a system" (204).

To the mainly cognitive and computational world of cybernetics, then, the theory of autopoiesis adds a strong focus on their structural coupling to the medium as the energetic world in which their living unfolds. As Varela notes, "[n]atural systems are under a constant barrage of perturbations, and they will undergo changes in their structure and eigenbehavior as a consequence of them" (*Biological Autonomy*, 205). Although the autopoietic system's cognitive reality is based on computation and observation, therefore, it is at the same time immersed in the energetic medium and involved in complicated biological processes that delimit the field of its ability to respond to and interact with that world and the other entities, such as animals, plants, molecules, and cells. In fact, the world and the infinite variety of autopoietic entities in it might be said to be one and the same thing.

In terms of biology, the level of cells is especially important because while physicists operate by default on atomic levels and chemists on molecular ones, biologists operate on cellular levels. "The cell is the smallest unit of life" (Margulis, 24). It is the "smallest autopoietic structure known today, the minimal unit capable of incessant self-organizing metabolism" (61). Cells are, "as indispensable basic systems of life operationally closed, i.e. 'autopoietically' organized" (Luhmann, *Soziologische Aufklärung*, 38). As "all living beings [...] perceive" (Margulis, 32), a cell already perceives and "is conscious" (122). In actual fact, "[m]ind and body, perceiving and living, are [...] self-reflexive processes already present in the earliest bacteria" (32).

Although their operational and informational organization defines humans as unities—"in the context of the assembled system, the autopoietic unity functions in such a way that the observer would describe it as allopoietic" (Maturana, *Erkennen: Die Organisation*, 214)—they are "in actual fact" composed of a large number of smaller autopoietic systems, all of which have different levels of structural complication. In terms of cognition, these smaller autopoietic systems function as partial observers.

From this perspective, humans are no longer completely human. Rather, they are assemblages of an infinite number of heterogeneous, both human and non-human, both material and immaterial series that are organized in a specifically human manner. Assemblages of bodies and habits. Similarly, animals are made up of an infinite number of heterogeneous series, both material and immaterial, organized in what we call a specifically animalistic manner. Because of specific evolutionary dynamics such as co-evolution, some of these series are compatible and can be plugged into each other. This happens, for instance, in the case of companion species, or, which might be the same, really, in the case of species that entertain symbiotic or parasitic relationships.

This recursive assemblage theory has caused Félix Guattari to ask whether supra-individual aggregates such as families or nations might also be considered as autopoietic. He raises this question in relation to his own notion of a general machinism. Should autopoiesis be restricted to the level of "living machines" (*Chaosmosis*, 34) or can social systems or flows of concrete be considered as living organisms? Yes, Guattari notes, proposing that Maturana and Varela's "notion of autopoiesis—as the auto-reproductive capacity of a structure or ecosystem—could be usefully enlarged to include social machines, economic machines and even the incorporeal machines of language" (93). What Guattari calls a "machinic autopoiesis" (37) "view[s] autopoiesis from the perspective of the ontogenesis and phylogenesis proper to any mechanosphere *superposed* on the biosphere" (40, emphasis added).

This superposition expands autopoiesis from biological machines to technical and social machines. Every autopoietic entity, Guattari argues—from single cell to city—emerges from an anonymous machinic multiplicity that provides a field of intensive potentiality. Even though it is informationally and operationally closed, every living being remains immanent to this field. "It is out of this chaos that complex compositions, which are capable of being slowed down in energetico-spatio-temporal coordinates or category systems constitute themselves" (59). "All there is" is born from the foam of this machinic chaos.

Although modern biology has detected forms of self-reflection in non-human autopoietic systems, let me, if only for purely operational and pragmatic reasons, maintain a formal distinction between human and non-human forms of self-reflection. Within the diversity of autopoietic systems, humans are defined by having developed a level of what Maturana and Varela variously call self-reflection, self-consciousness, or simply "observation." While all autopoietic systems share the property of cognition in its extended sense, and while all of them are reflexive, only some are reflective in the sense of having a built-in level of systemic self-reflection that allows them to see, experience, and talk about themselves as objects. In other words, what we call consciousness allows them to observe themselves.

Like second-order cybernetics, the theory of autopoiesis maintains that any organic "eigenlife" partakes of an operational and informational separation between itself and its outside. To draw a distinction between inside and outside is inevitable for any mode of individual life. In the words of Maturana, "[w]hen a space is parted, a universe comes into existence" (*Erkennen: Die Organisation*, 180). Only systems that are informationally and operationally closed can be said to also have a world, in contradistinction to being part of the world or making up part of the world.

In *Laws of Form*, George Spencer-Brown had used a similar image for the creation of his logical calculus: "The theme of this book is that a universe comes into being when a space is severed or taken apart. The skin of a living organism cuts off an outside from an inside. So does the circumference of a circle in a plane. By tracing the way in which we represent such a severance, we can begin to reconstruct, with an accuracy and coverage that appears almost uncanny, the basic forms underlying linguistic, physical, and biological science, and can begin to see how the familiar laws of our own experience follow inexorably from *the original act of severance*. The act is itself already remembered, even if unconsciously, as our first attempt to distinguish different things in a world where, in the first place, the boundaries can be drawn anywhere we please. At this stage the universe cannot be distinguished from how we act upon it, and the world may seem like *shifting sand beneath our feet*" (v, emphasis added).

In *The Embodied Mind*, Varela echoes Spencer-Brown—as well as Friedrich Nietzsche's seminal essay "On Truth and Lies in a Nonmoral Sense"—when he notes that "[o]ur journey has now brought us to the point where we can appreciate that what we took to be solid ground is really more like shifting sand beneath our feet" (217). As with Schrödinger's cat, the distinction between medium and form starts when a first formal discrimination cuts into the continuity of the undulating "waves of sand." As Luhmann notes, "every mathematical calculus [*Kalkül*] [...] is based on the fact that a differentiation [*Unterscheidung*] is made that marks a difference between the one and the other side. Such differentiation draws (and crosses) the border between an [...] unmarked state and a [...] marked state" ("Dekonstruktion", 269).

Cognitively, any differentiated and differentiating system can only operate from within one side of such a discrimination: "the operative use of the form can only proceed *from one of its sides*" (Luhmann, "Paradoxie," 245–246, emphasis added). In other words, any living system draws, or, again more correctly, is the result of the drawing of a border between inside and outside. As Spencer-Brown notes, "[a] distinction is drawn by arranging a boundary with separate sides so that a point on one side cannot reach the other side without crossing the *boundary*. For example, in a plane space a circle draws a distinction" (1, emphasis added).

The various processes of creating borders cause complex relations between insides and outsides, amongst them those between inside data and outside intensities: "We may also note that the sides of each distinction experimentally drawn have two kinds of reference. The first, or explicit, reference is to the value of a side, according to how it is marked. The second, or implicit, reference is to an outside observer. That is to say, the outside is the side from which a distinction is supposed to be seen" (69). Ultimately, "knowledge [*Erkenntnis*]" is "only possible [. . .] if and because systems close themselves operationally by way of their differentiations [*Unterscheidens*] and namings [*Bezeichnens*] and thus become indifferent to what is thus excluded as environment [*Umwelt*]" (Luhmann, "Erkenntnis," 239).

This formal constructivism calls for an "eigenepistemology" that is developed from within the cognitive system and that operates by way of the parameters of that system. Already von Foerster had asked "'[c]ouldn't we and shouldn't we find an *eigendescription* that is structured so that it describes itself?' That is the eigenvalue problem of life" (*Beginning*, 61, emphasis added), calling the result of such an epistemology an "eigentheory:" "'If we now want to solve the problem of a theory of knowledge, which means to create an epistemology, then it has to be one that explains itself, or in Hilbert's language, that is an eigentheory. [. . .] Experience is the cause | The world is the effect | The epistemology is the rule of transformation" (*Wissen*, 368–369).

An eigentheory creates values by identifying eigenvalues in the world that are the results of its own eigenbehavior. These values are created by way of the gradual stabilization of concepts through feedback loops between perception and world, between processes of integration and landscapes of intensity. In this light, Schrödigner' wave function is part of a true eigentheory. It is in this sense that Richard Feynman stated "[w]here did we get that [Schrödinger's equation] from? It's not possible to derive it from anything you know. It came out of the mind of Schrödinger" (chapter 16, page 20).

On this backdrop, Maturana and Varela's challenge is also "to understand the regularity of the world we are experiencing at every moment, but without any point of reference independent of ourselves that would give certainty to our descriptions and cognitive assertions" (*Tree of Knowledge*, 241). In one of von Foerster's trademark aphorisms, "objectivity is a subject's delusion that observing can be done without him" (Poerksen, 148). All knowledge, then, is based on self-referential, dynamic architectures of perceptual, cognitive, and observational differentiations that take place inside of the autopoietic system: "everything that is produced or reproduced as knowledge [*Erkenntnis*] needs to be reduced to the differentiation of differentiations [*die*

Unterscheidung von Unterscheidungen] (in difference to: to a 'ground')"
("Luhmann, Erkenntnis," 227).

In reference back to the question of how far complementarity can be
said to be ontic, an eigentheory can never claim to be complete or true
in any objective sense. Reality can only be "as it is observed." As Bateson
notes, "perception operates only upon difference. All receipt of
information is necessarily the receipt of news of *difference*, and all
perception of difference is limited by thresholds. Differences that are
too slight or too slowly presented are not perceivable. [...] Knowledge
at any given moment will be a function of the thresholds of our available
means of perception" (*Mind and Nature*, 29).

Again, in terms of knowledge, the relation between the living entity
and its medium is not defined by the flow of information between the
two poles, which was the position held by representatives of the realistic
theory of perception, and, according to Schrödinger, by classical physics.
Rather, the autopoietic system operates itself as a distributed network: "a
complex network of interacting elementary calculators [...] autonomous
in the sense that, being endowed with a spontaneity of its own, it is itself
the source of its own determining characteristics and not a simple
transducer converting input messages into output messages" (Dupuy,
553). The theory of autopoiesis, then, conceptualizes the world of
cognition and observation without recourse to any form of essentialism
or objectivism. The autopoietic system is "an 'autonomous' dynamic
system, informationally and organizationally closed, with neither input
nor output" (552).

"All of this" is correct, however, if and only if input and output are
defined in terms of information, internal operation and thus
epistemology. In the world of lived reality and in terms of energetics,
there are a multiplicity of contacts, because the system continually
interacts with the milieu's multiplicity of intensities. It is in addressing
these ontic and ontological levels that the theory of autopoiesis intersects
with the conceptual vector that the notion of eigenvalue draws through
the various fields it traverses.

Apart from providing a conceptual vantage point from which to
understand the constructedness of a psychic reality that is formed within
the system by processes of differentiation and integration—"*Forming*
[*Formsetzung*] *is* [...] *differentiating*" (Luhmann, "Paradoxie," 245)—the
theory of autopoiesis also conceptualizes a "lived reality" that concerns
the relation of the eigenorganization to the irritating and stimulating
world it lives in. This world is not an objective other but rather a landscape
of intensities to whose dynamics the system is energetically open.

All living systems that are operationally closed and energetically open to the world have membranic borders, skins, and receptor surfaces. As Margulis notes, "[a] membrane is a precondition for cell metabolism" (67). These membranes, however, do not need to be surfaces in a strictly topological sense and they do not even have to be material. They can be any perceptual machine that functions as a surface of sensation, such as the "skin-ego" proposed by Didier Anzieu. Even language, as a surface of sense, might be considered as a receptor surface.

When intensities impinge upon the system, they are experienced as irritations that cause structural changes in the system. Rather than sets of information that need to be read or decoded, they are causes for interior structural effects: "[A]n external agent acting upon a living system does not and cannot specify what happens in it as a result of its action. Such an external agent can only trigger in the living system a structural change determined in it. An external agent, therefore, does not and cannot be claimed to constitute an input for the living system because it 'tells' nothing to the living system about itself or about the medium from which it comes" (Maturana, "Autopoiesis, Structural Coupling and Cognition," 24).

The multiplicity of contacts between entity and medium creates an ecology of structural couplings and "congruent structural changes" (16) that is truly symmetrical, because "[t]he same happens as the living system impinges upon the medium: the living system can only trigger in the medium a structural change determined in the structural dynamics of the medium, and cannot be properly claimed to be an output of the organism because it 'tells' nothing about itself to the medium. It is in this sense that I claim that a living system does not have inputs or outputs, and that its relation with the medium cannot be described in informational terms" (24). This relation of structural coupling concerns both the living being—a "living system flows in its living in a path of the conservation of structural coupling [...] until the living system dies" (24)—as well as the medium. In terms of ecology, one might say, a medium also "flows in its living in a path of the conservation of structural coupling with living systems until it dies."

Apart from this symmetry, the quotes stress in particular the impossibility of living systems to immediately or directly touch the world in terms of information and operation. If one remembers that "objects" are the result of the specific eigenbehaviors of an observer, the nervous system ultimately cannot distinguish between a perception and a hallucination, since both are patterns of neural excitation. As Luhmann notes, "[a]t the level of the system's own operation there is no ingress to the environment, and environmental systems are just as little able to take part in the autopoietic process of the operationally closed system" (*Gesellschaft 1*, 49).

It is part of the operational organization of human beings, however, to habitually mistake the phantasmatic cognitive images they create of the milieu—the environment [*Umwelt*], that is—for the milieu. In Luhmann's terminology, they operate "under the illusion of having contact with the environment—at least as they only observe *what* they observe and do not observe *how* they observe" (*Gesellschaft 1*, 50).

This second-order observation—a term that is modeled directly on the term second-order cybernetics—denotes the level of the observation of observing systems. Such systems observe themselves as not having a direct relation to their milieu although they think they do. The reason for thinking that is that it facilitates their operation. Imagine how obstructive it would be to constantly think about the fact that one's reality is constructed. How much more practicable would it be to assume that real objects exist in the outside world? One might in fact argue that, in terms of evolution, the agency of first-order observation was invented to allow complex, reflective systems to act without too much cognitive interference, which is what second-order observation is all about. As if the unconscious was the system's invention against too much consciousness in the way "just living" might be said to be set against a too much of media studies.

The environment, then, denotes both the unconscious and conscious images and concepts humans construct *of* or extract *from* the medium that surrounds them. As Maturana notes, "[t]he medium of a unity is always defined by the unity as the domain in which it operates as a unity, not by the observer. The observer specifies a unity by an operation which implies an organization in the distinguished unity if it is a composite one, but the operation of distinction does not characterize the implied organization. Under these circumstances it is the implied organization of the unity that defines its medium, not the operation of distinction performed by the observer. Therefore, when an observer distinguishes a unity he does not necessarily have access to the medium in which it operates as a unity, but he himself defines a domain in which he sees the unity as a separable entity. The domain in which an observer sees a unity as a separable entity I shall call the *environment* of the unity" ("Cognition," 36–37).

Although they live inside a world, entities that are merely reflexive do not have concepts of that world. All they have are images *of* "their" world. That is, they have an "eigenworld." While they do have the faculty of the imagination, one might say, they lack an aesthetic sense as the "theory of the imagination." In fact, the role of the imagination is to ensure the operational misreading of intensive operations as informational operations. Without the imagination, reflective systems would be unable to interact pragmatically with their milieu because they would only see singular, unrelated parts. As if they were standing too close to a pointillist painting. The imagination allows living beings to see the world as more than a collection of intensive irritations, while the faculty of observation allows humans to develop the operational illusion that the images created by the imagination are in fact "the real things."

Although the theory of autopoiesis is an eigentheory, it does not reduce its investigative scope to the level of human observation and to the categories of thought. The recursion of the plateaus of autopoiesis implies that although information levels below the linguistic one are often treated as allopoeitic, they are not. Second, although the medium does not provide a landscape of knowledge, its "givenness" is crucial in terms of the autopoietic system's lived reality and thus the insistence of the categories of life in the categories of thought.

If the field of intensities is often eclipsed in Maturana and Varela's formalisms, which seldom address the field of given intensities *as* intensities, this is because their research concerns the organization of and the informational operations within the autopoietic system rather than the specific forms of perturbations that come to the system from that outside. The field of intensities, however, is not at all irrelevant in terms of their theory of structural coupling. Although the autopoietic system is informationally and operationally closed-off from the medium, this medium is the domain within which the system has assembled itself in the first place and to whose intensive continuum it remains immanent even while it has separated itself from it in terms of operation and information. In the theory of autopoiesis as well, science will always trail that intensive world with which it is entangled behind.

Even though the system is informationally closed off from the medium, it is everywhere in resonance with it. In fact, perception and cognition are highly tenuous, constantly shifting operations that are in many ways dependent on, and in interaction with, the intensive milieu. As Varela notes, if "perceptual activity cannot be so simply analyzed into a straightforward sequence, then it becomes difficult to separate the 'low' level of form from the 'higher' levels of, say, sensations or discernments (. . .). If we take the notion of a heap or pile (*skandah*) as a metaphor for the emergent configurations of a neural network, we will be led to think of the aggregates as resonant patterns in one moment of emergence" (*Embodied Mind*, 8).

Even Luhmann, who is not interested in the intensive medium *per se*, acknowledges that "the establishmnet and maintenance of system boundaries—including those of living beings—presuppose a continuum of materiality that neither knows or respects these boundaries" (*Gesellschaft 1*, 54). In other words, although an autopoietic system cannot exist without a medium to which it is immanent—"a unity exists in a medium determined by its properties as the domain in which it operates as a unity. Anything that a unity may encounter as a unity is part of its medium. Anything from which a unity may become operationally cleaved through its operation as a unity, is part of its medium" (Maturana, *Cognition*, 36)—this given medium is excluded from the system's observed world; from its "environment," that is, which denotes the medium as "given as given" rather than as "given."

The autopoietic system is thus defined simultaneously in two separate domains that follow divergent logics. Maturana calls these domains those of behavioral and structural change respectively: "the realm of interactions, in which behaviour is observed, and the structural realm, in which structural changes happen are related orthogonally, so to say, [. . .] and create fields of phenomena that do not intersect" (*Erkennen: Die Organisation*, 20). Accordingly, he differentiates between the human *being* as a living entity, which means as a "purely zoologically defined being" (*Was ist Erkennen?*, 95) and as "[h]omo sapiens sapiens*" (95). While the zoological entity (*zoe*) exists in the space of unrelational irritations, "[t]he 'human' [exists] in relational space" (95) (*bios*).

In topological terms, the systemic differentiation between inside and outside is a field in which inside and outside are separated, while in the field of intensity, inside and outside are not separated. As I noted, in terms of operational and informational closure, autopoietic systems are, in terms of relational operations, finite. At the same time, they partake of the infinite connectivity of the medium's intensive continuum.

In *The Embodied Mind*, Varela addresses the paradox that consistencies are embodied in the medium even while they are operationally and informationally separated from it in terms of what Schrödinger had considered to be an antinomy about the perception of color. "If we actually measure the light reflected from the world around us, we will discover that there simply is no one-to-one relationship between light flux at various wavelengths and the colors we perceive areas to have" (160). In the radical difference between "perceived color and locally reflected light" (160) it is the apparatus of visual perception that changes the optically measurable "surface reflectance" (167).

Varela's answer to Schrödinger's antinomy is that despite the fact that perceived colors are different from the intensive givens—the electromagnetic wavelengths measured by an objective, trivial technical apparatus such as a camera or a spectrometer—there is a resonance between the consistency and its medium that is not about the extraction of an objective truth or a stable reservoir of knowledge from the medium. Rather, it concerns an enacted correspondence. In this context, the designation of color functions as a communal, pragmatic value that is, in terms of evolution, useful to negotiate the relation between autopoietic systems as well as between an autopoietic system and its medium. It is an evolutionarily tested mode of non-trivial navigation within the optical world. "Our perceived world of color is (...) a result of one possible and viable phylogenetic pathway among many others realized in the evolutionary history of living beings" (183).

Other autopoietic systems operate according to completely different "viable phylogenetic pathways," such as the whale, whose wondrous optical view of the world Herman Melville marveled at in *Moby Dick*, or the compound eyes of certain insects. Each species translates quantitative stimuli into qualified perceptions. While the latter are created inside of each non-trivial entity, the comparability is provided by the similarity of the single entities of the species and the fact that the quantitative stimuli provide an identical intensity to which the single perceptions "correspond," or are "adequate."

As every eigensystem is immanent to the intensive medium within which it is actualized, its mode of perception cannot be modeled, as it was in classical versions of the cognitive sciences, on a "trivial" computational logic, such as the digital system of the computer. As Varela notes, "the manipulation of symbols after the fashion of digital computers. In other words, cognition is *mental representation*: the mind is thought to operate by manipulating symbols that represent features of the world or represent the world as being a certain way" (8). The problem with this approach is that "[a] digital computer [. . .] operates only on the physical form of symbols it computes; it has no access to their semantic value" (41). Computational models, therefore, cannot adequately answer the question of "[h]ow do the symbols acquire their meaning" (99).

In other words, how are intensities turned into data? Apart from not taking into account the relation between the analog and the digital, the computational model does not take into account that perception is spread out through the system and thus has to do "with how the system is put together, and, moreover, with how it perceives itself, in the sense that its own entanglement is the key to understanding what will happen to it" (Varela, "Laying Down a Path," 51).

Moving away from cognitive theories that rest on a logic of representation, Varela models cognition as embodied and enacted. Patterns emerge spontaneously within "adaptive resonant neuronal networks" (*Embodied Mind*, 96) and result in "a global state among *resonating neuronal ensembles*" (96). Varela actually states that "it seems difficult for any densely connected aggregate to escape emergent properties" (90). As he notes, "connectionist models are much closer to biological systems" (92) than computational ones: "Instead of *representing* an independent world, they *enact* a world as a domain of distinctions that is inseparable from the structure embodied by the cognitive system" (140).

In aesthetic terms, a theory of cognition must be expressive rather than representational. "To understand that neural processes form a nonrepresentational point of view, it is enough to just notice that whatever perturbation reaches from the medium will be in-formed according to the *internal coherence* of the system. Such perturbation cannot act as 'information' to be processed" ("Laying Down a Path," 60). As Varela describes it quite beautifully, "[i]t is not a mirroring of the world, but the *laying down* of a world" (62).

The challenge for cognitive science is thus to think of complex digital systems as the result of emergent processes, and to conceptualize the digital, representative, and symbolic plateau as a result and an attribute of pre- or subsymbolic, analog operations. "Since this global state emerges from a network of units that are more fine grained than symbols, some researchers refer to connectionism as the 'subsymbolic paradigm.' They argue that the formal principles of cognition lie in this subsymbolic domain, a domain above but closer to the biological than to the symbolic level of cognitivism. At the subsymbolic level, cognitive descriptions are built out of the constituents of what at a higher level would be *discrete symbols*" (*Embodied Mind*, 100, emphasis added).

In terms of set-theory, the symbolic level of cognition is a subset of the subsymbolic level from which it emerges. "[T]he most interesting relation between subsymbolic emergence and symbolic computation is one of *inclusion*, in which we see symbols as a higher-level description of properties that are ultimately embedded in an underlying distributive system" (101). Once the digital is understood as a subset of the analog, the symbolic, ideational level can no longer be operationally separated from the subsymbolic level. Already Bateson noted that data are digital representations of analog processes. As such, symbols are fundamentally both clear and "false." In Deleuze's words, they are "obscure because clear." "[T]he Idea is necessarily obscure in so far as it is distinct, all the more obscure the more it is distinct" (*Difference and Repetition*, 146). It is thus in being clear and distinct that difference is by necessity obscure. Or, put even stronger: In being difference, difference is by necessity false. This is ultimately what Deleuze means when he talks of the "powers of the false" in *Cinema II: The Time-Image*. While they are extremely powerful tools, all data are differential and thus "false," which is why they cannot be taken "at face value; they are seen as approximate macrolevel descriptions of operations whose governing principles reside at a subsymbolic level" (*Embodied Mind*, 102).

The distribution of data in the brain is materially decentralized, because "[i]n actual brains there seem to be no rules, no central logical processor, nor does information appear to be stored in precise addresses. Rather, brains can be seen to operate on the basis of massive interconnections in a distributed form" (85). This is why "any symbolic level becomes highly dependent on the underlying network's properties and peculiarities as well as bound to its history" (102). In the cognitive sciences' attempt to model this ecology of cognition, it must take seriously the differences between analog and digital, between formation and information, as well as between digitalized and digitalizing systems. It must address, in other words, the interplay between symbolic and subsymbolic—what Varela calls "subpersonal" (51)—cognition; between conscious and unconscious, imperceptible cognition. Between what Peirce calls "cognitive" and "perceptual" judgments.

If, in terms of media studies, the analog is defined as the quantitative and the digital as the qualitative and their logic is considered as infinitely scaled, the analog is "simply" that which a specific registering device cannot differentiate or has not yet differentiated. One might have to differentiate, therefore, between an ideal state of pure chaos or multiplicity, and a state in which chaos and order interact. Between what Deleuze and Guattari called the Plane of Immanence and the Plane of Consistency or "Plane of Consistencies."

In *Schizoanalytic Cartographies*, Guattari describes the initial chaos as "a place in which nothing referred to anything so as to refer to everything, at such a speed that nothing remains of these references" (119). Temporally, this is a state without memory, or, rather, in that state, the duration of memory "equals zero" (119). Paradoxically, each memory is infinitely short. Informationally, the state of chaos is a state without redundancy. A state of noise and semiotic turbulence that equals infinite information and thus infinite complexity. This plane is the cause of both an "ontological heterogeneity" (61) and an "ontological intensity" (29). All "complex compositions" (59) are born from within the "foam"—the "powdery diversity" (111)—of this chaos.

This infinitely multiplicitous, uneigen state is the "given" within which "the world" occurs, and that which anything that occurs trails behind. It is what Guattari had called the "aerosol of immanence." As I noted, however, the pure, uneigen chaos and the world's eigenchaos are complementary. From within a one-sided topology, which is the topology that is adequate to the logic of complementarity, the "two" would in fact have to be thought, somewhat paradoxically, as each other's "other side."

As the pure chaos as pure medium does not stop traversing the Planes of Consistency—as well as the Planes of Composition that denote the Planes of Consistency considered as actively composed by the consistencies on it—all forms remain immanent to that medium. In other words, every Plane of Consistency and of Composition will trail the chaos of the Plane of Immanence behind. As Guattari maintains, "beneath the diversity of beings, no unicoval ontological plinth is given" (*Schizoanalytic Cartographies*, 58). In every Plane of Consistencies or "Plane of Eigenvalues," a state without eigenvalues marks that plane's infinite potentiality of change. Within each form, a state without form. Within each form, a medium. Or, from the "other side" and perhaps more intriguingly, within each medium, a form.

Chapter 5

LITERARY STUDIES: 1906–1911, 1927

For a theory of color and light, as well as for the practice of painting, the importance of the theory of optical eigenvalues is immediately evident. What, however, about the theory of eigenvalues of and in language and literature? Are there eigenvalues in language? If there are, by what parameters are they defined?

In second-order cybernetics and the theory of autopoiesis, the function of language and its eigenlogic is not to represent the world, but to bring about a meaningful resonance between entities that have co-evolved within this world. If sound is the medium of sense, language is its form.

If the use of language does not rely on the computation of information coming to it from the outside, it must consist of operations of the mutual observation of entities within their medium and the respective integration of these observations into data. In the case of language, these are linguistic data. Language, then, is the mode of eigenbehavior that allows to make "distinctions of distinctions" and to contrast and compare these distinctions. As von Foerster notes, "two subjects that interact recursively [...] develop stable eigenbehaviors [*Eigenverhaltensweisen*], which must seem to be, from the point-of-view of an observer, communicables [*Kommunikabilien*] (signs, symbols, words etc.)" (*Wissen*, 279–280).

Language, then, is a linguistic code that organizes communicative actions. It can, as von Foerster defines it "as an emergent pattern of behaviour and thus as an eigenbehavior, be understood as a strange attractor or better as a constructive transactor that melts two autonomies into one" (*Wissen*, 298). In an article dedicated to Luhmann, von Foerster maintains that "[t]he word 'behavior,' as well as 'conduct,' 'action,' etc., does imply the recognizability of regularities, of 'invariants' in the temporal course of the action. [...] These invariants, these 'Eigen behaviors' arise through the recursively reciprocal effect of the participants in such an established social domain. [...] Communication is the Eigen behavior of a recursively operating system that is doubly closed onto itself. The essential thing about the topology of a double closure is that [...] through the hetarchical organization that comes with it, the fascinating possibility exists of allowing operators to become operands and operands to become operators" (*Understanding*, 322). In terms of human evolution, language is an important factor, although it is not a necessary element to survive. "I would say that language is just such an eigenvalue, an eigenbehavior. We speak—and it works perfectly. But there are *many* eigensolutions" (*Beginning*, 25–26).

As a consensual linguistic formation of the medium of sound, linguistic communication produces knowledge about the world that helps entities to adequately navigate their milieu. As Maturana and Varela state, we do not use language, therefore, as much as "we are in language [...], we 'language' only when through a reflexive action we make a linguistic distinction of a linguistic distinction. Therefore, to operate in language is to operate in a domain of congruent, co-ontogenetic *structural coupling*" (*Tree of Knowledge*, 210, emphasis added).

This is why language, which emerges "between" the multiplicity of the structural couplings that define the overall autopoietic system, is intimately linked to the biological phylum: "The moment and the context of the emergence of a communicative behaviour are not chance events, they are caused by the structural isomorphism of the communicating organisms and similarly by their structural coupling to the medium in which they exist" (Maturana, *Erkennen: Die Organisation*, 291).

Although language is the consensual eigenbehavior that defines observers, it is, at the same time, attributed to a field of intensities. As Maturana notes, differentiating between the physics and the metaphysics of language, "language is a biological phenomenon because it results from the operations of human beings as living systems, but it takes place in the domain of the co-ordinations of actions of the participants, and not in their physiology or neurophysiology. Languaging and physiology take place in different and non-intersecting phenomenal domains. Or, in other words, language as a special kind of operation in co-ordinations of actions requires the neurophysiology of the participants, but it is not a neurophysiological phenomenon" ("Reality," 45).

Language is thus not a tool humans use, but one element of an ensemble of eigenbehaviors that define humans. "When a metadomain of descriptions (or distinctions) is generated in a linguistic domain, the observer is generated. Or, in other words, to operate in a metalinguistic domain making distinctions of distinctions is to be an observer. An observer, therefore, operates in a consensual domain and cannot exist outside it, and every statement that he makes is necessarily consensual. [. . .] *An observer operates in two nonintersecting phenomenic domains. As a living system he operates in the domain of autopoiesis. As an observer proper, he operates in a consensual domain that only exists as a collective domain defined through the interactions of several (two or more) organisms"* ("Cognition," 45, emphasis added).

At this point, the logic of eigenvalues enfolds language as "the medium of cognitive observation" as well as living. It concerns both psychic memory and the structural memory that stores the structural couplings between the consistency and its milieu. Varela relates this "historical formation of various patterns and trends in our lives" (*Embodied Mind*, 116) to "what Buddhists usually mean by *karma*" (116). In both registers, the consistency's past leads up to its present and defines its abilities to avail itself of the milieu's potentiality.

The literary genre that aligns these two forms of memory is what Wilhelm Dilthey, who introduced the notion of eigenvalues into literary studies and whose use of the term had sparked off this investigation, calls the selfbiography. After 1904, the literary, the scientific, and the philosophical discourses form a superposition. Between 1906 and 1911, Dilthey develops the theory of the selfbiography. In 1927, the year Dilthey's essay is published, Schrödinger develops the ψ-function. In 1919, Heidegger develops, in direct reference to the notion of "eigenhood," the theory of the specific historicity [*Geschichtlichkeit*] of both actual and virtual life.

For Heidegger, the genesis of the notion of historical peculiarity lies in German Idealism. Johann Gottfried Herder saw "[t]he independent, ownmost value [*Eigenwert*] of each nation, each age, and any historical appearance in any sense". In fact, he maintained that the category of "ownness [*Eigenheit*]" is "related to all shapes of life." (*GA*, *56/57*, 133). Friedrich Schleiermacher "saw for the first time the ownmost being [*Eigensein*] and ownmost value [*Eigenwert*] of the community and of life in the community, as well as the peculiarities [*das Eigentümliche*] of the Christian community" (134).

The Heidegger of *Being and Time* from 1927 had developed much of his thought about "factical" or "inauthentic existence [*das uneigentliche Existieren*]" (BT, 354; SZ, 387) and about "*inauthentic* historicity [*uneigentliche Geschichtlichkeit*]" (BT, 354; SZ, 387) both with and against Dilthey. Although he would become increasingly critical of Dilthey's method, their projects revolve equally around the relation between factual and fictional history, which is somewhat misleadingly translated as that between "*authenticity*" (40) on the one hand and "*inauthenticity*" (40) on the other, while the German originals, *Eigentlichkeit* and *Uneigentlichkeit* (43) refer back directly to the logic of eigenhood.

For Dilthey, as for the theory of autopoiesis, the conceptual frame is how unconscious, intensive, and systemic histories that define structural changes are related to the measurement and notation of these histories in language as the cognitive platform responsible for behavioral changes. How can an intensive, unconscious history, and a cognitive, conscious history be aligned? In both cases, the question is how to think Félix Guattari's programmatic statement, which mirrors Maturana's statement that "*everything is said by an observer*" ("Everything is Said," 65; see also *Erkennen: die Organisation*, 34), that "[t]*here is no language in itself*" (*Machinic Unconscious*, 27).

Famously, the genre of the autobiography, or in today's terminology of "life writing," is based on a pact between writer and reader that is sealed by the writer's proper name [*Eigenname*] on the cover of the book. It focuses on the human being's contemplation of its factual course of life, or, in scientific terms, on the computation and measurement of its physical and psychic eigenvectors and eigenvalues. In fact, in terms of the logic of quantum theory, the telling of single events in an eigenbiography might be considered as measurements of the told life span, or, in other words, as that life span's "collapse".

Although Dilthey is clearly and exclusively concerned with the humanities, his investigation proceeds from a scientific account of the formation of biological systems and of systems of knowledge. In Dilthey's philosophy of life, the autobiography aims at bringing biology and psychology—in Deleuze's terms contraction and contemplation—into artistic resonance and thus to make them respond to each other.

Before I get to the autobiography proper, let me sketch the extent to which the theories I have dealt with are prefigured in Dilthey, whose account of hermeneutics feels almost like a prequel to much of what I have been talking about up until now.

According to Dilthey, life, as both the source of consistencies and as that which is embodied in them, contains the registers of cognition: "The living unit creates cognition from within itself: It is a finality [*ein Letztes*] behind which we are not able to retreat, we cannot subject [*unterwerfen*] this vitality that we experience to understanding, comprehension, which reaches, as it were, behind it [*welches gleichsam dahinter greift*]" (*Schriften*, XX, 321).

The ultimate measure and horizon of any form of understanding is the living being as an entity that is contoured against an intensive multiplicity from which it has emerged and to which it remains immanent. According to Dilthey, the beginning of philosophy lies, quite literally, in the pre-philosophical energy of an anonymous life that is embodied in a human being. Indeed, this claim forms the conceptual ground of Dilthey's philosophy of life: "The beginning of all philosophizing lies in the 'I,' in the originary energy of that I, by way of which it continually creates itself [*sich beständig setzt*]" (73). This "given energy," however, is not an essence in the classical sense. Rather, it is an anonymous, dynamic multiplicity, which is why "every attempt [...] to derivate the I from a unity is futile" (74).

From this ontological multiplicity, Dilthey develops a notion of individuality that is defined by the reciprocal presupposition of the fields of energy and intensity on the one hand, and those of cognition and thought on the other. In what reads like a direct rewrite of Friedrich Nietzsche's essay "On Truth and Lies in a Nonmoral Sense," Dilthey poses the categorical conceptual separation of the physical and the metaphysical, of quantity and quality, or, as he calls it, of the physical and the psychological: "*The process in which Sensation* [Empfindung] *develops.—The physical process*: the sense organs meet only processes of movement [*Bewegungsprozesse*].—*The physiological*: The processes of movement in the nerves and the brain are completely different from the physical ones.—*The psychological*: the qualitative sensation is completely heterogeneous from all of these processes of movement.—What does subjectivity of sensation mean?" (20, emphasis in original).

Like Nietzsche, Dilthey differentiates between three separate domains: the physical movement registered by the senses, the nervous movement within the system, and the attributed or adequate mental movement. The first threshold is between exterior causes to interior processes of registration: "The physiologist, who up until now only confirmed the physicist, now concludes further: what is uncomparable is in fact [*überhaupt*] the external cause of the sensation and the sensation itself" (268). Like Schrödinger, von Foerster, and Maturana and Varela, Dilthey differentiates formally between the incomparable [*unvergleichliche*] levels of quantitative irritation and the qualitative sensation [*Empfindung*]. As von Foerster noted, "[w]e achieve the integration of perception through the *motorium* and the unification of movement through perception" (*Beginning*, 82). In von Foerster's terminology, this is a "double coupling" (82). Once more taking up the quantum-theoretical terminology, von Foerster notes that "the two areas, the qualitative and the quantitative perspectives, should be seen as *complementary*" (14–15, emphasis added).

One can see how deeply Dilthey is involved in the physical and physiological sciences of his day, and how radically he pushes these sciences to their point-at-infinity. Not only does he note the formally insurmountable gap between quantity and quality. In the rhetorical question "what does subjectivity of sensation mean?," he opens up the problematics of whether perceptions [*Wahrnehmungen*] can even be considered to be subjective. It is not the subject that has sensations, Dilthey argues. Rather, sensations make up the subject. Pre-individual, unconscious, singular, sensations [*Einzelempfindungen*] form an ungrounded ground from which complex, conscious, and individual clusters of sensations are assembled. In other words, conscious, clustered sensations emerge from unconscious, singular sensations: "perception rests on single sensations, these are unconscious processes" (*Schriften*, XX, 95).

As the sensorium and the mind are formally separated from the motorium, the sensational and self-reflective landscapes form a closed system: "Self-consciousness brings us the consciousness of an exterior world that is independent of us" (154). All we have is "a multiplicity [*Fülle*] of perceptions, my sensations, subjective through and through. Equipped with this and the logical faculty [*Vermögen*] we confront the world, and the question arises: Is there a conceptual cognition of reality [*des Realen*] at all, is there a procedure [*Verfahrensweise*] that allows me to penetrate towards [*durchdringen zum*] the object?" (34). As for Luhmann, for Dilthey there is no direct "access to reality."

As only subjective sensations and logical reasoning remain from the quantitative world, Dilthey's question is rhetorical. In tune with quantum physics, Dilthey maintains that one can never reach a true outside reality, because that reality is radically constructed on the inside. In fact, already Dilthey considers objects to be merely tokens of a system's eigenbehavior: "materiality is nothing but resistance [*Widerstandsfähigkeit*] by way of the probing hand. Matter is nothing real, it is merely the creation of the sense of touch" (53–54).

What, however, about "reality"? At the same time that reality is cognitively constructed, the intensities of the external media multiplicity keep impinging on the subject as dynamic sets of physical pressures. Dilthey calls this, quite beautifully, "the pressure of the world on the subject" (*Selected Works, III*, 264). In fact, the system itself is nothing but a consolidated set of strategic resistances to these pressures: "The external world expresses itself in life as pressure through the relation of impulse to resistance" (352).

One of the most important implications of Dilthey's philosophy is that these pressures and stresses exerted by physical forces are the ultimate carrier-media of psychic life. In other words, all of psychic life is invariably embodied. In Dilthey's words, "[t]he life of spirit manifests itself on the base of what is physical" (217). While one might read this to mean that physical life forms the ontic plinth to psychic life, Dilthey stresses in particular the degree to which psychic life is at every moment in touch with and attributed to the changing intensities that trigger structural changes in the system: "[O]ur feeling of life [*Lebensgefühl*] [...] is continually caused by what resists and acts [*wirkt*] beyond our body [*Leib*]" (*Schriften*, XX, 173). As immanent to the circumstances, each individual life is deeply, and literally so, circumstantial.

Dilthey conceptualizes the split that defines the individual in topological registers as "the law of the many-sidedness [*Mehrseitigkeit*] of life" (328). One side is the "natural side of our existence" (326). Individual life realizes itself in multiple feedback loops with the complex milieus formed by the media into which it is suspended: "The individual existence of single persons unfolds into an infinite richness of life on the basis of their concerned relations [*Bezüge*] to their environment, to other people, and to things" (*Selected Works*, III, 156).

On the cognitive side, this quantitative variety of life is assembled and, again quite literally, qualified, inside of and by the living system: "*The exterior is given to me in the bustle* [Gewimmel] *of objects and people, which continually surround us and which we position into the external space* [in den Aussenraum verteilen]" (*Schriften*, XX, 175).

In this context, two questions are of particular interest for hermeneutics, both of which have to do with thresholds. The first question concerns a spatial threshold: "Where do exterior stimuli become internal ones? Here as well, the threshold fluctuates. Science can only state that where there is a nervous system, there is sensation" (123). The second question concerns a temporal threshold: "What does perception mean? We can only take in [*auffassen*] a single moment, all other processes are given to us only in memory" (55).

Both of these questions—What is the relation between the quantitative intensities and the qualitative sensations of life? What is the relation between the lived, or, as Dilthey calls it the experienced moment and the remembered moment?—are thrown into particularly sharp focus in the genre of the autobiography, which, from within aesthetic registers, triangulates the complex relation between the living entity, its systemic history, and its modes of self-expression and self-reflection. In terms of second-order cybernetics, the writer of an autobiography observes not so much other entities, but rather performs a self- or an eigenobservation in which the entity treats "itself" as an "other:" self- or autobiography as "eigenbiography."

After Dilthey's death, his editor, Bernhard Groethuysen, found an envelope amongst his writings that had a note attached to it. Here is Groethuysen's full account: "The manuscript on experience [*das Erleben*] was in an envelope [...] On the envelope, at the top, the following statement is written: "Life is a part of life in general [*überhaupt*]. But this is what is given in lived experience and cognition. Life in this sense thus extends over the whole scope of the objective spirit, insofar as it is accessible by way of lived experience. Life is thus the basic fact [*Grundtatsache*] that must form the beginning [*Ausgangspunkt*] of philosophy. It is what is known from within; that, beyond which one cannot go. Life cannot be brought before the juridical bench [*Richterstuhl*] of reason" (*Schriften*, *VII*, 359, not included in *Selected Works*, *III*).

The "Manuscript on Experience" [*Manuskript über das Erleben*], which Groethuysen calls "Das Erleben und die Selbstbiographie" (359), is the very essay in which Dilthey uses—only a few years after Hilbert had introduced the term into mathematics—the term eigenvalue, which in the English translation of Dilthey's work is unfortunately rendered as "distinctive value" or "inherent value."

As I noted, it is difficult to ascertain whether, and if, to what extent Dilthey relied on Hilbert's use of the term, although Dilthey's many scientific references, as well as his repeated use of mathematical models, make a direct connection quite plausible. Still, there are other conceivable backgrounds for Dilthey's use of the term, such as Kant's *Grounding for the Metaphysics of Morals*, which, in its differentiation between beings who have "ends in themselves" and beings who can be used as mere "means" has become, as I noted in my introduction, the main source for the common meaning of eigenvalue as "intrinsic value" in opposition to "use value."

What makes Kant a less plausible source for Dilthey than Hilbert, however, is that Kant does not use the term eigenvalue—in this context, today's use of the term is a back-projection onto Kant—and the fact that Dilthey's use of the term goes well beyond Kant's differentiation between intrinsic value and use value. Although my reading of Dilthey will thus proceed from the subjunctive condition of a direct influence, regardless of whether Dilthey knew of Hilbert's use of the term or not, there are intriguing resonances with Hilbert's use.

The immediate context of Dilthey's reference to eigenvalues is the description of the life (*bios*) that underlies the autobiography (*graphein*).

As Dilthey notes, much like rays of electromagnetic radiation, "[t]he intrinsic values [*Eigenwerte*] experienced in, and only in, the lived experience of the present are accessible to experience in a primordial way [*das primär Erfahrbare*] but they stand juxtaposed to each other without any connection. For each of them arises in the concern of a subject for an object accessible to it in the present. [...] Thus the intrinsic values [*Eigenwerte*] of the experienced present stand juxtaposed and unconnected; they can only be assessed when they are compared with each other. Anything else described as valuable must be referred back to intrinsic values [*Eigenwerte*]" (223). In this quote, Dilthey creates the formal paradox of a fractal multiplicity of eigenvalues: Eigenvalues "up to infinity."

Dilthey differentiates between these two series in relation to the temporal parameters of the present and the past. In developing an appropriate temporal logic, Dilthey operates with two modes and two adherent models of time, which are roughly equivalent to Henri Bergson's notions of *temps* and *durée*. The first, formal, and mathematical model of time is that of an infinitely dense succession of temporal moments or instants (*temps*). On the mathematical backdrop of the "Dedekind cut," Dilthey illustrates this model by way of the infinite subdivision of a continuous line by cuts, with each "present" or "instant" conceptualized as a mathematical and thus extentionless point that is identical to any other point. "If we think of time in abstraction from what fills it, then its parts are equivalent to each other" (*Selected Works*, 93), Dilthey notes.

If this time is the abstract time of "being," the second model is that of a concrete, embodied time and a constant "becoming." Its milieu is the "content of the lived experience" (93) as something that "constantly changes" (93). As it relies on the continuity of a duration [*durée*] that pertains to the spaces between the cuts that mark the infinitely dense succession of instantaneous presents ["*ist*"], this time is not captured in the chronological succession of the purely formal and mathematical cuts.

Whereas abstract, mathematical presents have no extension and no experienced duration, embodied, perceived presents do. This is why eigensystems have no direct cognitive access to the instantaneous presents, except, of course, as an abstract, mathematical, and thus ideal conceptualization. In fact, even the smallest subdivided moment of embodied time is, or has—somewhat like the Ψ-function between measurements—a specific duration. In another paradoxical conceit, Dilthey notes that in the continuity of embodied time "even the smallest part is linear; it is a sequence that elapses. There is never an *is* in the smallest part" (93).

If one defines an event as the smallest loosely coupled element of experienced time, and thus considers events as the temporal medium of perception, events do not lie in the infinitely small, arrested instant of a pure present—in their primordial experience, that is—but in the "filling of a moment of time with reality" (93), in the opening up of a pure, instantaneous present to a duration, however short that duration might be or might be thought to be. Even the shortest durational present, therefore, is suspended between a past and a future. Unlike abstract mathematical time, embodied time is a "[c]oncrete," "real," (94) and "actual [*wirkliche*]" (*Schriften*, *VII*, 72) time.

As the chronological medium of perceptual, mnemonic, and cognitive processes, this durational time is not the time of infinitesimally short, equidistant instants or fractions of being, but of processual and relational becomings. In Dilthey's words, it is always, even in its smallest modulations and continuous variations, a "course [*Verlauf*]" (94). Its spatial modality is invariably linear—as in "like a line"—which makes it inherently historical rather than punctual and instantaneous. It is the time of a constantly and continuously changing world. Of a world in change. As Cramer notes, "[t]he world does not exist, it happens [*sie ereignet sich*]" (*Symphonie*, 22).

This internal split within time creates the paradox that although "we always live in the present" (*Selected Works*, 94), we cannot perceive or experience this present. "Since the present never is, and even the smallest part of the continual advance in time contains the present and a memory of what was just present, *what* is present as such is never experienceable" (94). Invariably, the single moment of being is both "comprehended" and "stretched out" by a durational becoming. As they are durational, embodied presents "become" within memory: "The present never *is*; what we experience as present always contains the memory of what has just been present" (216). Again, although the pure present of mathematical, lived time and the duration of perceptual, experienced time operate simultaneously, epistemologically they operate on separate plateaus. Somewhat paradoxically, mathematical time is both the most abstract and the most corporeal of the two modes of time, as it can designate both extensionless ideality and the material pulses of a purely corporeal time. It is, in Maturana's terms, "zoological" time, whereas durational time is the time of relationality. *Temps* charts a time of physics, *durée* that of metaphysics. *Temps* is actual time, *durée* virtual time. *Temps* is quantitative time, *durée* qualitative time.

This twofold definition of time also concerns the difference between the perceiving system's physical and psychic plateaus, which are also both aligned and at the same time radically separated. For Dilthey, the system's physical and energetic coherence—its organic "course of life" (216)—is processual and continuous in the sense that it denotes the life of an entity within its structural envelope: "the existence of a person during his lifetime. The property of *uninterrupted constancy* belongs to that existence" (93, emphasis added).

Entities are continuous in that they have an overall organic and conceptual eigenvalue. At the same time, they are constantly changing and in flux. In fact, according to the theory of eigenvalues, they gain their consistence by maintaining a systemic invariance within the overall flux. However, as their perception and experience is based on integrations of this flux, that flux can never be perceived: "We experience both the changes in what-just-was and that such changes are occurring, but we do not experience the flux itself" (217). This is the fundamental paradox in and of process philosophy.

The entity's physical course of life consists of the "true" accumulation of single, lived moments and actions into a larger systemic history, in which the system's life is defined as a continuous process with an overall, "more or less invariant" eigenvalue and eigenstate. The succession and accumulation of lived instants makes up a systemic coherence that the human being quite literally is—the history of its structural couplings within an intensive ecology—as well as the value that defines the collective operations the entity performs and undergoes in the envelope of its operational space and time.

The zoological continuity and the creation of an overall zoological eigenvalue, however, do not necessarily imply the existence of what Dilthey calls an "ideal unity of the parts of life" (94), which is related to an entitiy's psychic rather than to its physical or zoological consistence, and which is restricted to conscious, observing entities. This ideal unity, in which single events—as the smallest modules of processual time in which one can identify specific eigenvalues—are integrated into an increasingly complex and large set, is the overall "meaning" (94) of a specific life.

In terms of a perceptual synthesis, which integrates series of single events into sequences of individual memories, each moment adds up to a line of psychic continuity. This relational continuity, however, is radically different from the zoological continuity of the specific course of a life. As Dilthey stresses, "[b]ut *independently thereof*, there is an experienceable connection [. . .] quite independently of their succession in time" (93, emphasis added). Giving meaning to life, then, consists of bringing its zoological, organic "matter-of-fact" course of life into resonance with an architecture of psychic, relational events.

In other words, the problem lies in correlating the system's zoological eigenvalue with its psychic eigenvalue and vice versa. "Each life has its own sense [*Sinn*]. It consists in a meaning-context in which every remembered present possesses an intrinsic value [*Eigenwert*], and yet, through the nexus of memory, it is also related to the sense of the whole" (221). Dilthey relates the construction of sense to the agency of the observer, who in the case of the eigenbiography comes to function predominantly as an "eigenobserver." In fact, Dilthey considers the eigenbiography as the literary medium *par excellence* in which an entity can contemplate this correlation—and its problematics—from a point of retrospective overview. In the eigenbiography, the entity couples the belatedness [*Nachträglichkeit*] of sense with the belatedness [*Nachträglichkeit*] of writing in order to regain a meaningful image of its own life: "Autobiography is merely the literary expression of the self-reflection of human beings on their life-course" (222).

It is in the context of this correlation that the term eigenvalue becomes important for Dilthey. If both physical and psychic eigenvalues remain invariant through the set of changes that the system undergoes, they come to define the system as a coherent and continuous aggregate. The set of psychic eigenvalues and thus psychic reality, however, is invariably linked and even attributed to the set of physical eigenvalues, and thus to physical reality; to the life behind which one cannot reach and that one trails behind.

If life forms the basis [*Grundtatsache*] of thought, the meaning and sense of a life lies in the relation of the coherence of one's organic course of life [*Lebensverlauf*] with an observed and constructed coherence. The writer of an eigenbiography narrates this course of life. This course, which is a constant flux, is perceived initially as a series of singular, unrelated micro-events each of which has its own eigenvalue because each moment, however short, has a specific duration. These eigenvalues, however, stand next to each other without "inherent relation."

The eigenbiography integrates these moments into a coherent, relational continuum to which an overall hermeneutical value or meaning can then be attributed. First, the point-matrix of single events is "automatically" integrated into larger sheets of memory. These sheets are then integrated into and organized by a retrospective narrative that creates the present value of the specific "system of life:" "a nexus that is determined by the relation of the significant moments of life to my present interpretation of it" (*Selected Works, III*, 95).

This narrated continuity allows one to give meaning to the subject's life as an organically coherent aggregate that reflects on itself. This meaning lies beyond both the quantitative processes of organic synthesis and the succession of single, lived instants with their specific eigenvalues. To become meaningful, perceived moments and their durations need to be qualitatively subsumed. Out of many smaller processes with their specific eigenvalues, the "autobiographical algorithm" creates the entity's overall psychic eigenvalue, which "it" then calls its psychic course of life: "Since, with the advance of time, that which has been experienced constantly grows and recedes ever more, memories of our own life-course are formed [. . .] In all these memories, some state of being is linked with its milieu of external states of affairs, events, and persons. An individual's life-experience results from the generalization of what has thus accumulated. It arises through procedures that are equivalent to induction. The number of instances on which the induction is based constantly increases in the course of a lifetime" (154).

Without the processes of inductive integration and imagination, the eigenvalue of each event would lie merely in its momentous relation to other events, which means that from the "point of view of value" (223), each life would consist of nothing but a multiplicity of unorganized and unvectored, singular events. Dilthey describes this state in terms of frequencies that make up "a chaos of harmonies and dissonances. Each of them is like a chord that fills a present, but they have no musical relation to each other [. . .] Only the category of meaning overcomes the mere juxtaposition or subordination of the parts of life to each other" (223). There are no eigenfrequencies in this multiplicity.

We are back, then, at the moment of the creation of a faint orientation within a multiplicitous vector-field. Somewhat like stochastically distributed photons are entrained into a strictly oriented laser beam, the eigenbiographical construction of the meaning of a life entrains single "events as eigenvalues" into a directed and directional—as in "vectored"—narrative. Both Cramer and DeLanda note a similar entrainment within sets of neurons or molecules. Operations in the brain, for instance, are based on the fact that neurons synchronize their impulses in a process Cramer calls "forced resonance" (*Symphonie*, 166). In fact, every entity is forced in this way because "an organism is assembled from a multiplicity of biorhythms with specific eigenfrequencies which must be in resonance [. . .] in order for the organism to function" (174) and "[a]ll *normal, stable systems* are superpositions of oscillations that are in resonance" (56).

Within this entrained or composed arrangement, "[t]he elements, the substructures, the subsystems are in turn vibrating [*schwingende*] systems with eigentimes [*Eigenzeit*]" (*Symphonie*, 80) and "eigenrhythms" (108; on the notion of eigentime in physics, see also Herman Minkowski and Albert Einstein, in whose theory of relativity the eigentime of an object is an invariant; more generally, see Luhmann (*Gesellschaft 1*, 83)). The integration of these moments into an overall coherence reduces and organizes the multiplicity of unrelated values into an overall harmonic set that encompasses all of the plateaus, from biological and chemical harmonies to the habit of thinking of oneself as a self. From intensities it creates values, from values, eigenvalues.

For humans, the successful correlation of physical eigenvalues with psychic eigenvalues ensures the coherence as a system that is formally split into the levels of physics and metaphysics. In terms of the eigenbiography, this alignment of physical and psychic reality relies on the ability to integrate, on all levels, lived life into the horizon of meaningful life. It is in this sense that cognition emerges from life, and that the eigenbiography emerges from lived intensity. In the words of Deleuze, "transcendence is always a product" and an attribute, one might add, "of immanence" (Immanence, 31).

Chapter 6

CULTURAL STUDIES: 2018

Niklas Luhmann has talked, somewhat paradoxically, of contingency as the eigenvalue of modern society to designate that era's structural spine. In a similar, if less paradoxical, manner, one might talk of the "eigenvalue of the baroque" or the "eigenvalue of colonialism." Perhaps one might even talk of the "eigenvalue of cultural studies." Beyond such general definitions, however, are there questions from within or about the field of cultural studies that the notion of eigenvalues might help to negotiate?

One seminal question in this regard is whether there are an adherent ethics and politics to the logic of eigenvalues. With the history of the notion of eigenvalue that I have traced in the preceding chapters in mind, can the default differentiation between *Eigenwert* and *Fremdwert* be re-evaluated? Let me propose a number of very preliminary ideas about that.

There is an ambiguity that runs through the term eigenvalue that plays itself out in a conceptual field spread out between the concepts of mathematical value and ethical value. Every existing entity has a specific mathematical eigenvalue. In both philosophical and political debates, this mathematical eigenvalue has been tied to an ethics that opposes this given eigenvalue to that entity's value "for someone else." In both senses of the word, therefore, any entity is inherently "valuable." In the case of humans, this has translated into having a number of inalienable rights that cannot be separated from the eigenvalued entity. Ultimately, both the political and the ethical discourse on equal rights are based on this strict coupling, despite the fact that throughout history, only carefully defined subsets of the overall set of entities were in actual fact granted equal rights. The disconnect is that to all other beings an ethical eigenvalue was denied although they had a mathematical eigenvalue. Already here, the notion of eigenvalue points toward an ethics that comprehends and protects all forms of individuated life.

That said, a more counter-intuitive proposition is that the true ethical value does not concern individuated life but the pure, anonymous life that runs through and "gives potentiality" to each and every eigenvalued entity. In terms of change, one might say that anonymous life consists of both psychic and physical movements that are uneigen, while individuated life consists of both psychic and physical eigenmovements. Which leaves a final paradox: ethical value lies precisely in that which has no eigenvalue—no mathematical value in itself, that is—but that pervades every entity as its potentiality to be and to change. It lies in that enigmatic something that we have to give a value to, both in terms of mathematics and ethics, in order to be adequate to it.

Both the weakness and the strength of "cultural studies as an eigenvalue problem" lies in this paradox, which calls for the development of an attitude toward the uneigen. Can this uneigen be defined? "No," in the sense that any definition is invariably an eigendefinition, which implies, as von Foerster had shown, that every definition is pragmatic rather than objective.

If it cannot be objectively defined, can one at least have an attitude toward it? An ethical position? "Yes." In fact, we all have, whether we realize it or not, an attitude toward the uneigen, because it is part of us as that which animates us and as that which is embodied, and thus qualified in and by us. In his essay "Immanence, a Life," Deleuze has isolated this uneigen life in the story "Our Mutual Friend" by Charles Dickens. A person who is unloved by most everyone seems to be dying. At the moment between life and death, all of his unpleasant characteristics [*Eigenschaften*] have been peeled away to reveal a pure life within him that shines forth in its anonymous, luminous splendor.

From this point of view, the uneigen can be read as a variation of a number of notions that philosophy has developed to conceptualize an ungrounded ground, such as "pure difference," "multiplicity," "pure change," or, in Guattari's words, a plane of "zero consistency" (*Schizoanalytic Cartographies* 106) as "the inexhaustible reserve of an infinite determinability" (103). A plane of "infinitely fast change." To posit such a ground for itself, for thought as well as for the world, does not entail to objectively define reality as such. It merely marks the point of perspective of the logic of the eigen. That logic of the eigen implies a logic of the uneigen.

There are, however, two aspects to that uneigen. In Schrödinger's terms, what I will call the quantitative eigenworld—the world before its measurement and evaluation, that is—does have an eigenvalue. It is just that this eigenvalue is a communal one. It is an eigenvalue that is, one might say, "smeared across reality." Here, the world's uneigenhood pertains to the collapse of its uneigenhood in the sense of its qualification by an observer. There is another state of uneigenhood, however, which is related more to Heider's notion of photonic multiplicity as pure luminosity. It is ultimately toward this given multiplicity that a belief in the value of the uneigen is directed. To value this multiplicity does not by itself solve any ethical problems and it is by no means a shortcut to utopia. It does lead, however, to an attitude that honors an anonymous, uneigen level of the world that cannot be qualified. According to a logic of complementarity that pertains between these two states—the eigenworld as a complex machinic arrangement of eigenvalues regardless of whether these are communal and quantitative or collapsed and qualitative, and the uneigen world of pure multiplicity—the uneigen world is indifferently also the eigenworld as that which is constantly qualified by "its" creatures and vice versa. This in both mathematical and ethical terms indifferent world is the ground of any form of what might be called "expressive eigenecology" as an ecology in which the world and its creatures mutually express each other.

If the uneigen world is unqualifiable, the quantitative eigenworld must be qualified, which is what Schrödinger meant when he noted that "there is no ψ-function in life." We are constantly collapsing the uneigen world. At every moment, we may stress either particle and collapse or wave and the ψ-function. Always, however, we should assume their complementarity and our being immanent to the field of the uneigen.

We are all attributes of and entangled in this quantitative world and what we feel are its beauties and cruelties. The quantitative world is not an overwhelming force outside of us but our milieu and medium. In fact, we, together with all of "its" other creatures, "make" this world—we qualify and embody it, that is—as we go along. The question is thus about how to organize the human part of that general qualification and embodiment. How to bring about qualifications and actions that are adequate to the realm of quantities. How to develop an "ecology of eigenvalues." In such a project, the quantitative, communal world provides an unmeasured measure to evaluate whether certain cultural operations respect this communal world.

One immediate universal currency of such an adequation might be the measure of pain. Although pain is an inevitable part of being a being in the world, the quantitative eigenworld does not feel pain. As von Foerster notes, "'out there,' there is no heat and no cold. There is a higher or lower average kinetic molecular energy [. . .] and certainly: 'out there' there is no pain" (*Understanding*, 233; see also *Wissen*, 56). The quantitative world feels "its" pain only through its creatures. It seems almost too easy—if it is so obvious, there must be something wrong

with it—to adhere to a maxim that proposes to always treat other
entities so that they do not suffer more than everybody suffers inherently
on a given scale of pain. This is easily said, but how to qualify
"unnecessarily?" How to administer pain?

Perhaps such a project needs an adherent ethics of sympathy, not as
in "compassion" but as in "sympathetic resonance." I think it would be
difficult to find arguments against such sympathy, other than to say that
things are obviously not so simple, which of course they are not. An
appeal to sympathy does not in itself produce sympathy, and the real
question is why, if the maxim is so convincing, it has never worked. The
answer to that question has not yet been found, and it probably will not
be found in the near or even the far future, although it lies at the heart
of theories ranging from psychoanalysis to economy and political
science. A more concrete question that is pertinent to the eigenvalue
problem is how comprehensively such a sympathy pervades reality? It is
in relation to that comprehensiveness that the notion of the uneigen
comes into its ethical own.

Let me propose a thought experiment [*Gedankenexperiment*]. If one
assumes that every eigenassemblage is pervaded by both uneigen
quantum states—the wave function considered as its unconscious, one
might say—as well as by an uneigen world, and if one further assumes
that the protection of that uneigen world and its mode of operation is
seen as the highest ethical value, a stone, a technical machine, or a pair
of jeans deserve as much respect as an ant, a child, or Dickens' grumpy
old man because we maintain similar dynamics of sympathy with all of
them. If the value of something lies in its link to the uneigen ground,
every form of qualified life—of sentient life, that is—should be equally
respected. There should be inalienable and equal rights for everybody
and everything. Certainly this counts for autopoietic systems but
perhaps for allopoietic systems as well.

We have to find, then, the threshold where strong irritation turns
into pain and we also have to accept that we cannot live without causing
pain. Who can say, in fact, how many living things each of us kills
unconsciously every day, from insects on windshields to jellyfish? How,
between vegetarianism and carnivorism, to develop a metabolic politics
and ethics that are adequate to the world?

Before getting caught up in these once more immensely complicated
and controversial questions, let me reverse the argument. Despite the
threshold between irritation and pain, should we not, given that the
notion of the value of the valueless defines all levels of reality, change
our relation to what we consider inanimate objects? Should we not

honor their eigenvalue even if they do not feel pain? Should we not feel sympathy or better: should we not honor the sympathy that always pertains? On the day we decide to treat inanimate objects ethically, which means, like we think we should treat "the living," the first thing that happens is that capitalism as we know it would break down. Immediately and irrevocably. We would not need a revolution. To treat objects as if they were part of the living—which, according to the logic of the uneigen, they of course are!—would be the revolution.

The notion of immanence, in the sense of being "inherent to" can help to conceptualize "how to be adequate to the world" and to understand why it would be a good thing. If taken seriously, a logic of immanence leads almost inevitably to an adequate attitude toward the quantitative and the uneigen worlds. Such a logic, however, needs to take immanence as comprehensive and as given, in the same way that sympathy is "given." Practices of immanence only work when, as Deleuze notes in "Immanence, a Life," "immanence is no longer immanence to anything other than itself" (27).

Again, it would be utopian to argue that to embrace a logic of immanence would solve the many problems we are faced with today. If these problems could be easily solved, chances are that they already would be solved, which is a lesson that pertains generally to what one might call "the problem of the world." As they are deeply entangled in that overall problem, many political and cultural questions are in fact so vast and intricate that one of the main problems is that of scaling: How to get from the level of global warming to the level of personally no longer using plastic bags and vice versa? Consider the difficulty of actually knowing whether, "all things considered," it might not be more ecological to use plastic bags than to use bags made from paper or hemp.

Precisely because there is no position of overview—we are within the problematics rather than without and there is no transcendental voice from the outside to tell us what to do—that to overcome these immensely complicated problems, one needs to develop, within the multiplicity of actors and agendas, an overall attitude toward the world. According to such an attitude, the choice between plastic and hemp is easy, one might say, although, "all things considered," it might in actual fact be the wrong choice. This should not deter one from choosing hemp, however, because nobody will ever be able to look at the problem in consideration of all things. In the light of the fact that it is impossible to "consider all things," my proposition is inherently a gamble. It opens up the question of how an attitude toward the world might be grounded.

If one maintains that the most viable choice is the one that is most adequate to the system of the world, what does "adequate," in this context, mean?

In *Difference and Repetition*, Deleuze proposes a figure of thought that contours the conceptual complexity of the logic of immanence. "Instead of something distinguished from something else," Deleuze notes, "imagine something which distinguishes itself—and yet that from which it distinguishes itself does not distinguish itself from it" (28). Deleuze illustrates this "unilateral distinction" (28) by way of the phenomenon of a lightning bolt that "distinguishes itself from the black sky but must also trail it behind, as though it were distinguishing itself from that which does not distinguish itself from it" (28).

The notion of being different from but simultaneously being a part of that from which one is different is, perhaps, the most general conceptual basis of such an attitude toward the quantitative, uneigen world. As singular beings, we distinguish ourselves from the world around us. Inevitably, however, we trail this world, which does not distinguish itself from us, behind. The uneigen world in its splendid, chaotic uneigenhood is the plane in which our living unfolds. If we honor this uneigen plane in its ceaseless change and diversity, we will, despite all of the constraints operative in our qualified eigenworlds, and despite the pains inevitably produced in them, honor change and diversity.

At the same time, it would be wrong to celebrate change as such. As we inevitably live within a world of ceaseless change, the question is rather how to administer that given change in such ways as to allow for maximum diversity. A change toward fascism is obviously a catastrophic change toward less diversity. The circumstances of change is why an attitude can never become a program. Rather, it is a pragmatic mode of dealing with an inevitably constrained life "with and without" the world. Perhaps it is enough to always attempt to act according to the logic of diversity as the logic that underlies the operation of the quantitative world and "its" reality. We need a politics and ethics for an eigenworld that trails the uneigen world behind. To modify a political rallying cry from the 1960s, "within the eigen and its vicissitudes, the uneigen." Within the system, the unsystematic. Within the paving stones, the beach.

CONCLUSION: LIFE

If the world consists of a multiplicity of eigenvalues, and if it is at the same time pervaded by the sheer potentiality given by a state without eigenvalues, then an ethics and a politics that honor the complementarity of the uneigen world and the eigenworld has never been described more clearly and more laconically, perhaps, than by Heinz von Foerster's "ethical imperative" (234) in *Wissen und Gewissen*. "Act in such a way that the number of possibilities of choice increases!" (234).

BIBLIOGRAPHY

Anzieu, Didier. *The Skin Ego*, translated by Chris Turner. New Haven, CT: Yale University Press, 1989.

Barad, Karen. *Meeting the Universe Halfway: Quantum Physics and the Entanglement of Matter and Meaning*. Durham, NC: Duke University Press, 2007

Barad, Karen. "Transmaterialities. Trans*/Matter/Realities and Queer Political Imaginings." *GLQ: A Journal of Lesbian and Gay Studies* 21, no. 2/3 (2015): 387–422.

Bateson, Gregory. *A Sacred Unity: Further Steps to an Ecology of Mind*. London: HarperCollins, 1991.

Bateson, Gregory. *Mind and Nature: A Necessary Unity*. Cresskill, NJ: Hampton Press, 2002.

Bell, J. S. *Speakable and Unspeakable in Quantum Mechanics*. Cambridge: Cambridge University Press, 1993.

Bergmann, Ludwig, and Clemens Schaeffer. *Lehrbuch der Experimentalphysik, Band 4. Bestandteile der Materie. Atome, Moleküle, Atomkerne, Elementarteilchen*. Berlin: de Gruyter, 2003.

Berressem, Hanjo. "'The Habit of Saying I': Eigenvalues and Resonances." In *Scientific Cultures – Technological Challenges. A Transatlantic Perspective*, edited by K. Benesch and M. Zwingenberger, 45–80. Heidelberg: Winter, 2009.

Berressem, Hanjo. "'Der *Eigen*name': Eigenwert und Eigenbiographie." In *Name, Ding, Referenzen*, edited by S. Börnchen, G. Mein, and M. Roussel, 131–151. Paderborn: Fink, 2012.

Binswanger, Ludwig. "The Existential Analysis School of Thought." In *Existence: A New Dimension in Psychiatry and Psychology*, edited by Rollo May, Ernest Angel, and Henri F. Ellenberger, 191–213. New York: Basic Books, 1958.

Bohr, Niels. "The Quantum Postulate and the Recent Development of Atomic Theory." Supplement to *Nature* (14 April 1928): 580–590.

Bohr, Niels. "On the Notions of Causality and Complementarity." *Dialectica* 2 (1948): 312–319.

Braun, Michel. *Differential Equations and Their Applications*. New York: Springer, 1983.

Bryant, Levi R. *Democracy of Objects*. Ann Arbor, MI: University of Michigan Library, 2011.

Castoriadis, Cornelius. *World in Fragments: Writings in Politics, Society, Psychoanalysis, and the Imagination*, edited and translated by David Ames Curtis. Stanford, CA: Stanford University Press, 1997.

Clarke, Bruce, and Mark Hansen, editors. *Emergence and Embodiment: New Essays on Second-Order Systems Theory*. Durham, NC: Duke University Press, 2005.

Cramer, Friedrich. *Symphonie des Lebendigen: Versuch einer allgemeinen Resonanztheorie*. Frankfurt am Main: Insel, 1998.

De Broglie, Louis. 1924. *Recherches sur la théorie des Quanta*. Doctoral thesis, University of Paris.

DeLanda, Manuel. *A Thousand Years of Nonlinear History*. New York: Swerve Editions, 2000.

Deleuze, Gilles. *Empiricism and Subjectivity: An Essay on Hume's Theory of Human Nature*, translated by Constantin Boundas. New York: Columbia University Press, 1991.

Deleuze, Gilles. "Postscript on the Societies of Control." *October* 59 (Winter 1992): 3–7.

Deleuze, Gilles. *Expressionism in Philosophy: Spinoza*, translated by Martin Joughin. New York: Zone Books. 1992.

Deleuze, Gilles. *Difference and Repetition*, translated by P. Patton. New York: Columbia University Press, 1994.

Deleuze, Gilles. "Immanence, a Life." In Gilles Deleuze and Claire Parnet, *Dialogues II*, translated by Hugh Tomlinson and Barbara Habberjam. New York: Columbia University Press, 2007.

Deleuze, Gilles. *Cinema II: The Time-Image*. London: Bloomsbury, 2013.

Deleuze, Gilles, and Félix Guattari. *What is Philosophy?*, translated by Hugh Tomlinson and Graham Burchell. New York: Columbia University Press, 1994.

Dilthey, Wilhelm. *Gesammelte Schriften, Band XX. Logik und System der Philosophischen Wissenschaften*, edited by Hans-Ulrich Lessing and Frithjof Rodi. Göttingen: Vandenhoek & Ruprecht, 1990.

Dilthey, Wilhelm. *Gesammelte Schriften, Band VII. Der Aufbau der geschichtlichen Welt in den Geisteswissenschaften*, edited by Hans-Ulrich Lessing and Frithjof Rodi. Göttingen: Vandenhoek & Ruprecht, 1992.

Dilthey, Wilhelm. *Selected Works, Volume III. The Formation of the Historical World in the Human Sciences*, edited by Rudolf A. Makkreel and Frithjof Rodi. Princeton, NJ: Princeton University Press, 2002.

Dirac, P. A. M. "On the Theory of Quantum Mechanics." *Proceedings of the Royal Society A* 112, no. 762 (1926): 661–677.

Dirac, P. A. M. *The Principles of Quantum Mechanics*. Oxford: Oxford University Press, 1930.

Dupuy, Jean-Pierre. "Philosophy and Cognition: Historical Roots." In *Naturalizing Phenomenology: Issues in Contemporary Phenomenology and Cognitive Science*, edited by Jean Petitot, Francisco J. Varela, Bernard Pachoud, and Jean-Michel Roy. Stanford, CA: Stanford University Press, 1999.

Feynman, Richard P., Robert B. Leighton, and Matthew Sands. *The Feynman Lectures on Physics, Volume 3. New Millennium Edition: Quantum Mechanics*. New York: Basic Books, 2011.

Foerster, Heinz von. *Das Gedächtnis: Eine quantenphysikalische Untersuchung.*
Wien: Franz Deuticke, 1948.

Foerster, Heinz von. "Cybernetics." In *Encyclopedia of Artificial Intelligence,*
edited by Stuart C. Shapiro, 309–312. New York: John Wiley & Sons,
1992.

Foerster, Heinz von. *Wissen und Gewissen: Versuch einer Brücke.* Frankfurt am
Main: Suhrkamp, 1993.

Foerster, Heinz von. *The Beginning of Heaven and Earth has no Name. Seven*
Days with Second-Order Cybernetics, edited by Albert Müller and Karl.
H. Müller; translated by Elinor Rooks and Michael Kasenbacher. New York:
Fordham University Press, 2014. *Der Anfang von Himmel und Erde hat*
keinen Namen. Eine Selbstschaffung in 7 Tagen. Berlin: Kulturverlag
Kadmos, 2002.

Foerster, Heinz von. *Understanding Understanding, Essays on Cybernetics and*
Cognition. New York: Springer, 2003.

Groethuysen, Bernhard. "Anmerkungen." In Wilhelm Dilthey, *Wilhelm Diltheys*
Gesammelte Schriften. Band VII. Der Aufbau der Geschichtlichen Welt in den
Geisteswissenschaften, edited by Bernhard Groethuysen. Leipzig: Teubner,
1927.

Guattari, Félix. *Chaosmosis: An Ethico-Aesthetic Paradigm,* translated by
P. Bains and J. Pefanis. Bloomington and Indianapolis, IN: Indiana
University Press, 1995.

Guattari, Félix. *The Machinic Unconscious: Essays in Schizoanalysis,* translated
by Taylor Adkins. Los Angeles, CA: Semiotext(e), 2011.

Guattari, Félix. *Schizoanalytic Cartographies,* translated by Andrew Goffey.
London: Bloomsbury, 2013.

Heidegger, Martin. *Sein und Zeit.* Tübingen: Max Niemeyer Verlag, 1953.

Heidegger, Martin. *Identität und Differenz.* Pfullingen: Günther Neske, 1957.

Heidegger, Martin. *Identity and Difference,* translated by Joan Stambaugh.
New York: Harper & Row, 1969.

Heidegger, Martin. *Die Grundprobleme der Phänomenologie. GA 24,* edited by
Friedrich-Wilhelm von Herrmann. Frankfurt am Main: Klostermann,
1975.

Heidegger, Martin. *Zur Bestimmung der Philosophie. GA 56/57,* edited by
B. Heimbüchel. Frankfurt am Main: Klostermann, 1987.

Heidegger, Martin. *Being and Time,* translated by Joan Stambaugh. Albany, NY:
State University of New York Press, 1996.

Heider, Fritz. "Thing and Medium." In *On Perception, Event Structure, and*
Psychological Environment: Selected Papers. Psychological Issues, Volume 1,
no. 3. Monograph, 1–35. New York: International Universities Press,
1959.

Heider, Fritz. "Ding und Medium." In *Kursbuch Medienkultur,* edited by
Claus Pias et al., 319–333. München: Random House, 2008.

Heisenberg, Werner. *Physics and Philosophy: The Revolution in Modern Science,*
translated by A. J. Pomerans. London: Allen & Unwin, 1959.

Helmholtz, Hermann von. *Die Lehre von den Tonempfindungen als Physiologische Grundlage fuer die Theorie der Musik.* Braunschweig: Friedrich Vieweg, 1863.

Helmholtz, Hermann von. *On the Sensations of Tone as a Physiological Basis for the Theory of Music,* translated by Alexander J. Ellis. London: Longman's Green & Co., 1895.

Hilbert, David. *Nachrichten von der Gesellschaft der Wissenschaften zu Göttingen: Mathematisch-Physikalische Klasse. 1.–6. Mitteilung,* 1904.

James, William. *The Works of William James, Volume 3. Essays in Radical Empiricism,* edited by Frederick H. Burkhardt, Fredson Bowers, and Ignas K. Skrupskelis. Cambridge, MA: Harvard University Press, 1976.

James, William. *The Principles of Psychology, Volume 1.* New York: Dover Publications, 1980.

Kant, Immanuel. *Grounding for the Metaphysics of Morals,* translated by James W. Ellington. Indianapolis, IN: Hackett, 1981.

Luhmann, Niklas. *Die Wissenschaft der Gesellschaft.* Frankfurt: Suhrkamp, 1992.

Luhmann, Niklas. "Kontingenz als Eigenwert der Modernen Gesellschaft." In *Beobachtung der Moderne,* 93–128. Opladen: Westdeutscher Verlag, 1992.

Luhmann, Niklas. "Deconstruction as Second-Order Observing." *New Literary History* 24 (1993): 763–782.

Luhmann, Niklas. *Soziologische Aufklärung 6: Die Soziologie und der Mensch.* Opladen: Westdeutscher Verlag, 1995.

Luhmann, Niklas. *Die Gesellschaft der Gesellchaft,* Band 1 und 2. Frankfurt: Suhrkamp, 1998.

Luhmann, Niklas. *Die Kunst der Gesellschaft.* Frankfurt: Suhrkamp, 1998.

Luhmann, Niklas. *Art as a Social System,* translated by Eva M. Knodt. Stanford, CA: Stanford University Press, 2000.

Luhmann, Niklas. *Aufsätze und Reden.* Stuttgart: Reclam, 2001.

Luhmann, Niklas. "Dekonstruktion als Beobachtung zweiter Ordnung." In *Aufsätze und Reden,* 262–296. Stuttgart: Reclam, 2001.

Luhmann, Niklas. "Die Paradoxie der Form." In *Aufsätze und Reden,* 243–261. Stuttgart: Reclam, 2001.

Luhmann, Niklas. "Erkenntnis als Konstruktion." In *Aufsätze und Reden,* 218–239. Stuttgart: Reclam, 2001.

Margulis, Lynn, and Dorion Sagan. *What is Life?* New York: Simon & Schuster, 1995.

Massumi, Brian. *Parables for the Virtual: Movement, Affect, Sensation.* Durham, NC: Duke University Press, 2002.

Maturana, Humberto R. "Cognition." In *Wahrnehmung und Kommunikation,* edited by Peter M. Hejl, Wolfram K. Köck, and Gerhard Roth, 29–49. Frankfurt: Peter Lang, 1978.

Maturana, Humberto R. *Erkennen: Die Organisation und Verkörperung von Wirklichkeit.* Braunschweig: Vieweg, 1982.

Maturana, Humberto R. "Everything is Said by an Observer." In *Gaia: A Way of Knowing: Political Implications of the New Biology*, edited by William I. Thompson, 65–82. Hudson, NY: Lindisfarne Press, 1987.

Maturana, Humberto R. "Reality: The Search for Objectivity or the Quest for a Compelling Argument." *The Irish Journal of Psychology* 9, no. 1 (1988): 25–82.

Maturana, Humberto R. *Was ist Erkennen? Die Welt entsteht im Auge des Betrachters*, translated by Hans Günter Holl. München: Piper, 1994.

Maturana, Humberto R. "Autopoiesis, Structural Coupling and Cognition: A History of These and Other Notions in the Biology of Cognition." *Cybernetics & Human Knowing* 9, no. 3/4 (2002): 5–34.

Maturana, Humberto R., and Francisco J. Varela. *Autopoiesis and Cognition: The Realization of the Living*. London: D. Reidel Publishing Company, 1980.

Maturana, Humberto R., and Francisco J. Varela. *The Tree of Knowledge: The Biological Roots of Human Understanding*, translated by R. Paolucci. Boston, MA: Shambhala, 1998.

Miller, Jeff, editor. "Earliest Known Uses of Some of the Words of Mathematics." Last modified September 2, 2016. http://jeff560.tripod.com/e.html.

Moretti, Franco. *Distant Reading*. Brooklyn, NY: Verso, 2013.

Naess, Arne. "Deep Ecology and Ultimate Premises." *The Ecologist* 18, no. 4/5 (1988): 130.

Naess, Arne. "The Deep Ecological Movement: Some Philosophical Aspects." In *Deep Ecology for the Twenty-First Century*, edited by George Sessions, 64–84. Boston, MA: Shambhala, 1995.

Neumann, John von. "Allgemeine Eigenwerttheorie Hermitescher Funktionaloperatoren." *Mathematische Annalen* 102 (1929): 49–131.

Nietzsche, Friedrich. "Über Wahrheit und Lüge im aussermoralischen Sinne." In *Friedrich Nietzsche: Sämtliche Werke. Kritische Studienausgabe, Band 1*, edited by Giorgio Colli and Mazzino Montinari. Berlin: De Gruyter, 1988.

Peirce, Charles Sanders. "Pragmatism and Abduction." In *Collected Papers of Charles Sanders Peirce, Volume V. Pragmatism and Pragmaticism*, edited by Charles Hartshorne and Paul Weiss, 180–212. Cambridge, MA: Belknap Press, 1965.

Peirce, Charles Sanders. "A Survey of Pragmaticism." In *Collected Papers of Charles Sanders Peirce, Volume V. Pragmatism and Pragmaticism*, edited by Charles Hartshorne and Paul Weiss, 317–345. Cambridge, MA: Belknap Press, 1965.

Peirce, Charles Sanders. "Design and Chance." In *Writings of Charles S. Peirce: A Chronological Edition, Volume 4. 1879–1884*, edited by Christian J. W. Kloesel, 544–554. Bloomington, IN: Indiana University Press, 1986.

Plotnitsky, Arkady. *Niels Bohr and Complementarity: An Introduction*. New York: Springer, 2013.

Poerksen, H. "Interview: At each and every moment, I can decide who I am: Heinz von Foerster on the observer, dialogic life, and a constructivist philosophy of distinctions." In Bernhard Poerksen, *The Certainty of Uncertainty: Dialogues Introducing Constructivism*, 1–28. Exeter: Imprint Academic, 2004.

Schöne, Wolfgang. *Über das Licht in der Malerei*. Berlin: Gebr. Mann, 1954.

Schrödinger, Erwin. "Quantisierung als Eigenwertproblem." Part I: *Annalen der Physik* 79 (1926): 361–376. Part II: *Annalen der Physik* 79 (1926): 489–527. Part III: *Annalen der Physik* 80 (1926): 437–490. Part IV: *Annalen der Physik* 81 (1926): 109–139.

Schrödinger, Erwin. "Die gegenwärtige Situation in der Quantenmechanik." Part I: *Die Naturwissenschaften* 48 (November 29, 1935): 807–12. Part II: *Die Naturwissenschaften* 49 (December 6, 1935): 823–828. Part III: *Die Naturwissenschaften* 50 (December 13, 1935): 844–849.

Schrödinger, Erwin. "Indeterminism and Free Will." *Nature* 138, no. 3479 (4 July 1936): 13–14.

Schrödinger, Erwin. "Mind and Matter." In *What is Life? With Mind and Matter and Autobiographical Sketches*, 90–165. Cambridge: Cambridge University Press, 1967.

Schrödinger, Erwin. "The Present Situation in Quantum Mechanics," translated by John D. Trimmer. In *Quantum Theory and Measurement*, edited by J. A. Wheeler and W. H. Zurek, 152–167. Princeton, NJ: Princeton University Press, 1983. Originally published in *Proceedings of the American Philosophical Society* 124, no. 5 (1980): 323–338.

Schrödinger, Erwin. "Quantisation as a Problem of Proper Values." In *Collected Papers on Wave Mechanics: Together with his Four Lectures on Wave Mechanics*, Third (augmented) edition. Providence, RI: American Mathematical Society, 2003. Part I: 1–12. Part II: 13–40. Part III: 62–101. Part IV: 102–123.

Segal, Lynn. "Appendix: An Interview with Heinz von Foerster." In Lynn Segal, *The Dream of Reality: Heinz von Foerster's Constructivism*, 135–148. New York: Springer, 2001.

Serres Michel. *Genesis*, translated by Geneviève James and James Nielson. Ann Arbor, MI: University of Michigan Press, 1982.

Serres Michel. *The Birth of Physics*, edited by David Webb; translated by Jack Hawkes. Manchester: Clinamen Press, 2000.

Spencer-Brown, George. *Laws of Form*. London: Allen & Unwin, 1969.

Stirner, Max. *The Ego and His Own*. New York: Harper & Row, 1971.

Varela, Francisco J. *Principles of Biological Autonomy*. New York: North Holland, 1979.

Varela, Francisco J. "Eigenbehavior: Some Algebraic Foundations of Self-Referential System Processes." In *Principles of Biological Autonomy*, 170–207. New York: North Holland, 1979.

Varela, Francisco J. "Laying Down a Path in Walking." In *Gaia: A Way of Knowing: Political Implications of the New Biology*, edited by William I. Thompson, 48–64. Hudson, NY: Lindisfarne Press, 1987.

Varela, Francisco J., Eleanor Rosch, and Evan Thompson. *The Embodied Mind: Cognitive Science and Human Experience*. Cambridge, MA: MIT Press, 1993.

INDEX